THE
GUMPERT
FOUNDATION

ISBN 978-0-9852971-7-6

Dialogues In Action

408 NW 12th Ave, Suite 506

Portland, OR 97209

503.329.4816

dialoguesinaction.com

Table of Contents

Dedication

As Trustees of the William Gumpert Foundation, we are pleased to present this compilation of your *Project Impact* evaluation reports. *Project Impact* is an eight-month program that helps nonprofits measure their programmatic impact, including the "beyond numbers" change they are creating. We are proud to bring these types of educational programs to the San Diego nonprofit community and want to both thank and commend the eleven outstanding organizations that participated in this challenging endeavor. We hope the many hours of thoughtful and diligent work you invested lead to a deeper understanding of your transformative impact and provide new ways to assess and communicate the results of your incredibly important, impactful work.

Patrick Dempsey & David Cornsweet

Introduction

Steve Patty, Ph.D.

The aim of *Project Impact* is to develop in nonprofits the ability to self-study their impact. As such, this is a capacity-building project. Over the past eight months, a cohort of eleven nonprofits from the San Diego area has met monthly for instruction and practice in evaluation.

The development of evaluation capacity takes time and iteration. It requires both instruction and practice – training in some of the leading techniques of research accompanied by ongoing applications and practice. This project recognizes the power of partnership, the enrichment of cross-pollination of ideas among like-minded organizations, the durable impact of a learning community, and the potential inspiration for a sector when exemplars are developed and elevated.

Project Impact takes teams of leaders from nonprofits through a process of discovery about the power of evaluation. The idea is to develop the ability to see and communicate the effects of the programs on the people they are designed to serve. There are three primary movements to the project: (1) Intended impact, (2) Inquiry, and (3) Implication.

Project Design

The project begins with a focus on the work of identifying and clarifying the intended impact of each of the participating programs. Once the ideas have been developed and indicators identified, the teams then design a questionnaire to collect data about quantitative measures and a qualitative interview protocol to collect qualitative data. These data are analyzed. Themes are identified and then translated into findings. From the findings, the teams develop program responses and communiques of their impact.

The fundamental elements of the Seeing Impact Project follow an arc of evaluation design:

Part 1 - Intended Impact

This project begins with the identification and clarification of what effects are intended through the work of each of the projects. Each team develops an articulation of intended impact to include the components necessary for evaluation design.

A. Main Ideas of Impact

Each team identifies and crafts ideas of impact to frame the intention of direct impact for the program. In some cases, these ideas are mapped in relation to the secondary and tertiary impacts of the program to gain clarity about the fundamental notions of desired effect as a direct consequence of the program or service rendered.

B. "What We Mean"

From these primary ideas, the teams then develop a brief explication of the meaning of their ideas of impact. This translates ideas that are occasionally technical and into messages accessible to all.

C. Quantitative Indicators (E3)

Teams then identify luantitative indicators for each of the ideas. The aim is to generate five or six of the most critical indicators for each idea, paying attention to the data power, proxy power, and communication power of each of the key ideas. As well, the intent in this step is to identify a range of cognitive, affective, and behavioral indicators that can be measured through metrics.

D. Qualitative Indicators (E4)

Teams also identify qualitative indicators in this stage. These indicators are articulations of the structural and qualitative elements of growth and development that signal progress toward key ideas of impact. The qualitative indicators become the basis for the protocol construction to inform the in-depth interviews in the inquiry phase.

Part 2 - Inquiry

In the inquiry stage of the project, each team designs and implements a strategy for data gathering. These take two forms: a questionnaire to collect quantitative data and an in-depth interview to gather qualitative data.

A. Quantitative Data and Analysis

For each of the E3 indicators, teams construct items for a questionnaire. Since these projects are not intended to provide experimental or quasi-experimental inquiry, the attribution of effect is built into the questionnaire items. The questionnaire is deployed, in most cases, to the entire population of recipients the program reaches. Data are analyzed mostly using measures of central tendency. The teams then design displays of the data and narrative for their report.

B. Qualitative Data and Analysis

The development of a qualitative design encompasses a number of steps, including the following:

1. **Protocol Design.** Each team designs an in-depth interview protocol that uses the *Heart Triangle*™ method of question design. These produces a protocol of about nine sequences of questions (18 questions in total) to be

used as a guide for seeking data about the awareness and reflection of subjects' structural shifts and developments of growth and progress.

2. **Sample.** Each team identifies a sample of subjects using a purposeful stratified technique to identify a selection representing of the population being served.

3. **Data Collection.** Interviews a convened, most lasting between 45 minutes and 1 hour in length. Data are collected via notes during the interview, and then augmented immediately following the interview to provide a substantive rendering of the interview.

4. **Data Analysis.** Team members apply a four-step model of analysis to each of the interviews. This process provides them with a casual version of coding and interpretation, illuminating the primary themes from each interview.

5. **Thematics.** Through a guided and facilitative process, the entire data corpus is then examined. Themes are mapped through meta-analysis of the emerging insights.

Part 3 - Implication

The intent of the project is not to leave teams simply with a report about their program's effects, but rather to use the insights from the evaluation to guide the further development of the program. This takes two forms:

A. Program Adjustments

The team then takes each of the findings from the evaluation and considers possible program adjustments informed by the discoveries of the evaluation. This keeps the evaluation relevant for program application and improvement.

B. Program Experiments

In addition, the teams work to identify potential design experiments that they might run as an implication of the insights gained through the evaluation.

In this stage, the teams also begin to develop a report of the evaluation findings as well as other possible communiques of their discoveries to staff, stakeholders, funders, and other members of the community.

Explanation of the Reports

The reports of the organizations are included in the following discussion. These include highlights from the three movements of the *Project Impact*. For each participating organization, there is an explication of the primary findings from the evaluation accompanied by the programmatic responses of strategy and design. Since each organization has unique strategy and ethos, each report exhibits unique character and personality. Each report also includes both "prove" findings (evidence of impacts being achieved) and "improve" findings (areas for attention and further development). These reports are windows into the effects of the work of these organizations in the lives of the people they serve.

Words Alive

Adolescent Book Group

Patrick Stewart
Executive Director

Chrissy Califf
Operations Director

Amanda Bonds
Senior Program Manager

Theresa Tolentino
Teen Services Program Manager

Executive Summary

The purpose of this report is to present the process Words Alive undertook and the findings discovered as we set out to measure the impact of our Adolescent Book Group (ABG) program.

Established in 1999, Words Alive was founded on the belief that if you value reading and understand its fundamental connection to all aspects of your life, you will thrive as a lifelong learner - *ready to transform your community.* In that vein, our mission is to open opportunities for life success through the power of reading, and with our three primary programs: Read Aloud, Teen Services and Family Literacy, Words Alive provides life-changing services to 5,500 at-risk students and families monthly.

As our flagship program, Adolescent Book Group (ABG) serves 450 at-risk teens, most of whom have been referred to specialized community schools by the Juvenile Court system and have experienced extraordinary circumstances such as violence, pregnancy and homelessness. Each month, Words Alive hosts integrative programming within alternative classrooms through book discussions, writing sessions and college/career readiness workshops. Through reading and sharing opinions about texts, ABG participants enhance self-esteem, reading levels, vocabulary, critical thinking and literary analysis.

As a means to continually provide meaningful and evaluation-driven programming, Word Alive commenced the seven-month Dialogues in Action (DIA) project to analyze our ABG program using both a qualitative and quantitative evaluation model. Through this process, we had an opportunity to view our program from a different perspective – through the lens of our students. Interviewing both ABG student participants and our teachers, Words Alive was able to examine the intended impact made in the classroom and determine resolutions in order to enhance our program delivery.

Our key program goals within ABG are as follows:

> ➤ Students develop an enduring commitment to reading.

> ➤ Youth become life-long learners.

> ➤ Youth become advocates for themselves.

Our key findings from both our qualitative interview process and quantitative survey include:

Sharpened skillsets: After participating in the ABG program, students are reading more efficiently and purposefully. Teachers reported that students – whom may have not read a book cover-to-cover prior to Words Alive – are now reading for comprehension, citing evidence from text to support their claim or opinions.

Boosted confidence: Students who participated in three or more sessions noted a sense of confidence in not only their literacy skills but also their communication with their peers, teachers and Words Alive volunteers. The practice of sharing ideas and perspectives of books enhanced students' comfort-level with reading aloud and discussing in a classroom setting.

Enhanced commitment to reading: As an aim to encourage students to become readers, through this process we learned that students are recognizing the important of literacy in their everyday lives – not just within the context of school.

Humanized reading: Students started to see themselves as readers and as part of a reading community.

Shifted attitude towards reading: Students' viewpoints related to books has transformed from a negative perception of reading to a positive one; students understand that reading isn't just a novel but rather a key component in their day-to-day lives.

Improved communication: Students are developing their own voice in order to better express themselves – in the classroom, amongst their peers and within their community.

Increased book ownership and access: Students are building their home libraries and sharing their love of books with others.

Enriched group learning: Students now have agency in their own education, working as a team to read a book, discuss, learn and prosper.

The following review is an insight to the interconnectedness literacy plays in our everyday lives. In effort to showcase the need for intervention, this document will address the importance of literacy-centric programming in order to support at-risk students and families in developing strong reading skills and habits. Studies have proven that literacy is at the heart of our community. As a means to advocate for oneself, literacy is the key to success – whether it's in regards to your professional career, educational pathway or daily responsibilities, like going to a physician or signing a rental agreement. Reading is a part of everything we do; it's integrated into our lives. This is the impetus behind the Words Alive program – it's our mission to make reading matter and change the landscape in San Diego County.

Words Alive & Why Literacy Matters

We read to learn, to experience our world and to advocate for ourselves — quite simply, to live full lives. In this way, literacy is a fundamental skill needed for life success, yet 450,000 San Diego County residents lack basic reading proficiency. At Words Alive, our goal is to change the story of children, youth and families in our community by fostering a love of reading, ensuring they won't be counted among that number.

We also know that literacy development starts early, and youth who struggle with reading are at a significantly higher risk for illiteracy and low-literacy later in life. Research has shown a strong connection between low-literacy and poor life outcomes, such as poverty, reliance on public assistance programs, underemployment and high risks of incarceration.

That's why our programs focus on connecting under-served populations with access to quality reading experiences, materials and a growing community of readers. Founded in 1999, Words Alive began with a singular vision to introduce at-risk teenagers to experiences of meaningful reading. Since then we have blossomed into a cornerstone of San Diego County's literacy movement. Today we serve 5,500 children, youth and adults each month through our three flagship programs and numerous community collaboration projects.

Adolescent Book Group

This impact report focuses on our Adolescent Book Group (ABG) program - an integrated, comprehensive language arts program delivering monthly book discussion groups in combination with a writing program, college and career readiness workshops and an annual arts component. Serving approximately 450-students each month, highly trained volunteers share their love of reading through interactive, directed discussion and writing groups. These sessions provide the students opportunity to develop their voice, express opinions about books, enhance their literacy skills and make connections between text and real life applications.

Our primary partners in this effort include 22-Momentum Learning classrooms (formerly Juvenile Court and Community Schools), a fully accredited educational program of the San Diego County Office of Education (SDCOE) for youth who are wards of the court or have been referred to alternative learning settings by social services, probation, or one of the 42-school districts in San Diego County. As an alternative learning setting, Momentum Learning classrooms specifically serve some of San Diego County's highest at-risk teens, many of whom are navigating considerable challenges, including transitioning in and out of the delinquency system, teen parenthood, living in foster-care, substance abuse and homelessness.

Intended Impact

In order to measure not just our outputs (what we did), but also our outcomes (what changed because of what we did), Words Alive participated in a Dialogues in Action (DIA) Project Impact cohort, measuring the impact of our programs along with crafting a meaningful narrative around both the quantitative as well as qualitative outcomes. Through this process, we've identified three-specific areas of intended impact:

Students develop an enduring commitment to reading. By this we mean that students internalize the value of reading as a tool and remain engaged in reading habits during and following their participation in the program.

Youth become life-long learners. By this we mean youth experience positive attitudinal shifts about learning and recognize their own ability to seek out information to solve problems; acquire critical thinking skills; and transition successfully into post-secondary education or career environments.

Youth become advocates for themselves. By this we mean youth find their voice and are empowered to invest in their futures. Youth will increase self-confidence as readers, writers and speakers; expressing themselves more clearly and strengthening their writing; make steps towards personal, educational and career goals; gain competency in navigating post-secondary education and career systems;

and pursue success through commitment to activities which lead to specific desired outcomes.

Methodology

The aim of our evaluation was to ascertain the type of effect our program has on the teen population we are serve within Momentum Learning. Over the course of seven months, our team developed and refined ideas of intended impact and indicators; designed and implemented both qualitative and quantitative means to collect and analyze data; and identified findings and implications for program adjustments and renovations.

This evaluative project commenced with an insightful analysis of our program and its impact on our students and classrooms. Once we had a clear understanding of our programmatic goals, we designed a questionnaire to collect data geared towards quantitative measurements for our entire Words Alive ABG population as well as hosted qualitative interview protocol with 26 students and eight Momentum Learning teachers. From our analysis, our team identified trends and translated into findings. From these findings, we developed program responses and communiques.

Qualitative Data and Analysis

Our qualitative approach followed these steps:

Protocol Design

We designed an in-depth interview protocol using the Heart Triangle method of question construction. This produced a protocol consisting of nine sequences of questions (22 questions for our student populations and 20 questions for our teacher population). The protocol was our guide to collect data about the subjects' awareness and reflection of structural shifts and developments of growth and progress. (See Appendix B for Interview Questions.)

Sample

We identified a sample of subjects using a purposeful stratified technique to select a representation of the population we serve. Our population size was 450 students and 22 teachers. From our population size, we decided to focus on schools with lower rates of student turnover in order to see the longer-term impact of students who participate in multiple sessions. From those school sites, we selected students who participated in three or more sessions, or 50% of the total program sessions offered during the school year. In addition to the number of sessions the students participated in, we drew our sample from the following strata of our population: 30% of students were female while 70% male (mimicking student demographics according to the 2014-15 School Accountability Report Card, the most recent report available).

Of the 450 students we served during the 2014-15 program year through the Adolescent Book Group, 111 or 25% of students attended three or more program sessions and, per our established protocol, were eligible for qualitative interviews. We interviewed 26 students, or 23% of students who had participated in three or more sessions at that time of the interviews. We also interviewed nine, or 41% of the 22 teachers participating in the program. The teachers interviewed represented all classrooms of interviewed students.

Data Collection

We conducted one-on-one interviews lasting between 45-minutes and one-hour in length. Data were collected via notes during the interview, and then recorded immediately following the interview to provide a substantive rendering of the conversation.

Data Analysis

We applied a four-step model of textual analysis to each of the interviews. This process allowed us to interpret the meaning and significance of the interview data.

Themes

We then examined the overarching themes that emerged from the full scope of our data analysis to illuminate the primary insights and discoveries. From our interviews, we discovered the following themes:

> Skills

> Confidence

> Commitment

> Humanizing effect

> Attitudinal shifts

> Communication

> Book Ownership and Access

> Group Learning

Quantitative Data and Analysis

We also designed a questionnaire to collect data on our quantitative indicators of impact. We sent this questionnaire to all 22 teachers to administer for our 450 students. Students were involved with standardize state testing at the same time we deployed the survey, which impacted the response return rate. We received 75-total survey responses, or 17% of the 450 sample. This sample size of 75 included students who participated in less than three sessions as well as students who participated in three or more sessions. By comparing both groups, we were able to see the differences between students that have received more Words Alive intervention as opposed to students who are newer to our programming.

The questionnaire is composed of 10 questions, regarding students' behavioral changes and their relationship to reading. (See Appendix C for questionnaire.) The data was analyzed primarily using measures of central tendency.

Our evaluation produced findings which captured the primary discoveries from the data. The most salient of the findings are described in the following narratives.

Findings

Finding 1: *"Doing More with What We Read"—Sharpening Skillsets*

By the end of the program, 100% of teachers interviewed not only reported that their students were reading more, they stated specifically that their students were doing more with what they read – that students were, in effect, flexing skills sharpened through months spent habitually reading, writing about and discussing texts. This was the most fundamental change we saw among students participating in the program.

Students noticed this too. As one student shared, "at first I didn't like reading because I didn't understand what I was reading, even though it was my level book. I would just go on and on to finish, and wouldn't know what I was reading."

When asked what changed, she replied, "I started paying attention. I learned how to get myself into a book, how to question what I'm reading to get into it. [Now] I get why readers are reading." In interviews, teachers on the other hand, repeatedly identified this change as getting better at reading for comprehension. Reading for comprehension, or the ability to process what we've read and understand, is a complex process for learners and improvement in this area speaks to positive changes in the skills needed to process, interpret and put a text in context within the world outside the story. In this vein, teachers reported observing increased student vocabulary, fluency, ability to annotate and analyze text, and use evidence to support their claims and ideas. One student provided a very specific example of building fluency, stating "I've overcome pronunciation, like 'acknowledgement' in Black and White. I knew what the word meant, but I'd never seen it written down. Then I saw it in Girl in Translation and I knew how to pronounce it really fast."

In general, students responding to the quantitative survey self-reported that participating in Adolescent Book Group improved their ability to express themselves as readers, writers and speakers. The chart below shows the percentage of students who identify a skill as strengthened via participation in the program. It is important to note that, as we anticipated and is shown below, students who attended at least half (3) of the offered program sessions during the school year positively identified sharpened skills more frequently than students attending the program fewer than three times.

Participating in the program has helped my ability to...

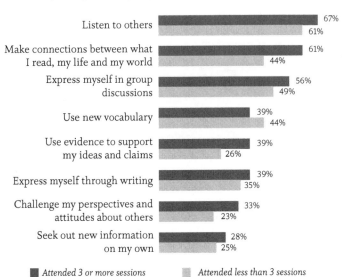

Listen to others	67% / 61%
Make connections between what I read, my life and my world	61% / 44%
Express myself in group discussions	56% / 49%
Use new vocabulary	39% / 44%
Use evidence to support my ideas and claims	39% / 26%
Express myself through writing	39% / 35%
Challenge my perspectives and attitudes about others	33% / 23%
Seek out new information on my own	28% / 25%

■ *Attended 3 or more sessions*　　▨ *Attended less than 3 sessions*

Significance

When students do not or cannot read for comprehension, motivation to read and self-confidence as a reader stalls, which in turn, deters students from the reading practice needed to strengthen their ability. It is a challenging cycle, but if we can interrupt that cycle with interventions like the Adolescent Book Group that engage students in increased time spent reading through methods that help them learn to pull meaning out of what they read, we open the opportunity for many of our other desired outcomes to develop and deepen.

It is well documented in research on literacy development in adolescents that skills, motivation or interest to read, and confidence as a reader work in concert to propel student ability forward. Imagine a snowball gaining momentum as it rolls down a hill. And this year, as students sharpened the tools in their belt, they saw what reading can offer them as a lens to their own world, providing a sense of relevancy of reading to their lives and relationships.

Our Response

Adjustments:

> Implement expository writing within monthly writing program sessions and/or book club discussions;

> Provide close readings of short/argumentative text;

> Enhance volunteer role and training to incorporate methods to read for comprehension, annotation, the importance of reading, interpretation and critical thinking.

Experiments:

> Employ small group pedagogy within monthly book discussion to highlight vocabulary, interpretation of text and use of evidence to support claims/ideas;

> Pilot 1:1 tutoring opportunities for students that are reading below grade level.

Finding 2: *"Students have come alive" — Gaining Confidence*

Hand-in-hand with sharpening skills, by the end of the program 100% of teachers interviewed reported growth in student confidence. Most immediately, students saw that they could, in fact, finish a book — for some, the first book they had ever finished in their lifetime–and student pride in getting through books reoccurred as a theme in student interviews.

Students were recognizing that they could do this, and each month as the pages turned, pens scribbled and discussions continued, teachers witnessed students taking risks in front of one another as well. This is where Words Alive staff, volunteers and partner teachers saw that growing skills and confidence was changing the learning dynamic in class and the caliber of the discussion. Students were, in effect, showing up differently for the program: we heard new student voices chiming in during discussions, witnessed others volunteer to read aloud or share a piece of their writing and, in a move of classroom leadership, step up to help facilitate book club discussions alongside volunteers or fellow classmates. As one teacher described it, "students have come alive."

In addition to gains in student confidence observed by teachers, students viewed themselves as better readers after the program. The chart below depicts, on a scale of 1-5, the percent of students who rated themselves a good (4) or very good (5) reader before and after participating in the program. Again, the data showed that students who attended more program sessions were showing greater gains. For example, 56% of students who participated in 3 or more sessions rated their reading ability higher on the scale as opposed to just 28% of students who attended less than three program sessions. Returning to our image of the snow ball rolling down the hill: the more you go, the more you grow.

Before and after comparison of students rating themselves as good or very good as a reader

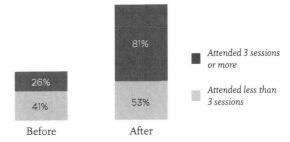

Significance

The lives of many students in the Adolescent Book Group program are scarred by crisis, failure, loss and missteps. These students are also bright, creative and remarkable survivors, but the circumstances of their lives often undercut their confidence as learners and their engagement in their learning environment. Thus, taking risks, especially in the role of learner and in front of their peers, is not a comfortable one. But with practice, engaging tasks and encouragement from consistent and caring adults, students develop the confidence to take a more active role in their own learning and support the learning environment of others.

Our Response

Adjustments:

➤ Enhance student facilitation process in the classroom by creating student-centric book discussions and ownership;

➤ Create more sharing opportunities, such as writing and/or project-based assignments.

Experiments:

➤ Establish protocol for student facilitation, such as grade adjustment, student/volunteer preparation and student role;

➤ Establish a speaker's bureau, designed to involved current and former Teen Services students in Momentum Learning and Words Alive outreach;

➤ Host college/career readiness workshops tailored to public speaking and expressing oneself.

Finding 3: *"Sticking with it to make it yours" — Commitment*

Our program aims to help high-risk teens become readers, and establishing those enduring reading habits starts with smaller commitments that develop a student's willingness or motivation to engage in reading. Our time in the classroom, paired with teacher and student interviews revealed three such commitments taking root:

1. Student commitment to themselves

2. Student commitment to their peers

3. Student commitment to volunteers

First, we noticed that students' dedication to reading varied depending on how long they participated in program. Specifically, students who attended sessions more often were more likely to finish the next book. Dovetailing on growing skills and confidence that they could get through a book, students with books under their belt were more likely to demonstrate a commitment to future books read in the program.

Additionally, students showed a commitment to reading and their peers by motivating each other to finish the books used in the program. A theme in teacher interviews described students in an exchange such as:

Student A: "Did you get to the part in chapter 10 where…"

Student B: "Don't say, I'm not there yet!"

Student A: "Well hurry up, or I'm going to spoil it."

Finally, students were impacted by the commitment of volunteers who visited their classroom to facilitate the program. As students and volunteers built rapport, and students learned that volunteers were not paid, but came of their own volition and interest to discuss books with the class, students upped their commitment to be prepared for discussion. In the words of one teacher; "It's different with the volunteers – it's not a school assignment. Students know they'll be coming soon and they want to have something to contribute when volunteers arrive. They're accountable to them in a different way." Simultaneously, during program sessions, students were observing people outside of teachers and administrators sharing their own love of and commitment to reading. Students are observing that reading is a real thing that real people do regularly - *and of their own volition.*

In select cases, where students were also young parents, they extended their commitment to the next generation by developing reading habits with their own children: one student shared, "Words Alive has helped me become a reader," going on to say that she now loves to read to her son, thus passing the torch and showcasing her commitment to reading as a model to her little one.

Significance

Students and teachers alike shared that student's viewed reading quite narrowly as something certain people do, in a certain place, for a certain reason – mostly that you read in school with teachers in order to graduate. Very often, this view was bolstered by home environments where students lacked the stability, materials and role-models that help reading routines take shape. Through the Adolescent Book Group however, students were developing confidence (believing they could do this), and fluency (knowing what their reading) and building commitments to themselves, each-other and adults who chose to be there as support along the way. Students were moving from reading as something they did, to a reader as someone they were.

Our Response

Adjustments:

> ➤ Work with Momentum Learning teachers and administrators to ensure the Words Alive programming is fully integrated into the classroom;

> ➤ Implement a mid-month check-in prior to the book discussion and writing program to encourage more participation amongst students.

Experiments:

> ➤ Align curriculum with Thematic Interdisciplinary Project Based Learning (TIP), Tutoria and/or ELA units to ensure program is integrated into the Momentum Learning curricula.

Finding 4: *"Seeing ourselves in one another" — The humanizing effect of sharing stories*

This sense of commitment, confidence and heightened skills-set was delivering students to a point of deeper reflection. Hence, another important theme in teacher and student interviews was connection – specifically as a sense of deepening empathy and a broadening world view. In discussion and in their writing, students were demonstrating that they were relating to stories, characters, their peers and volunteers and placing it in the context of our community. As one student explained:

> With the characters too, sometimes you can relate to how they are or their situation. The most recent book we read, Girl in Translation, I thought I was a lot like her and I saw how we had the same

thought or doubt, but we thought about it differently. Like how she didn't speak the language in school and dressed differently. I had a similar experience at school in Mexico, but I thought more about how the other kids saw me instead of focusing on my studies like she did. I wanted to know what happened to her. It changes the way you think about the world – there are certain things in the book where I was like wow, if the book hadn't told me about that I wouldn't have known.

Students were recognizing themselves in what they read - this certainly supported their interest in the books they were reading and, importantly, their motivation to get to the end. In interviews, students shared that when characters in the book that went through similar problems as they experienced, they felt more positive about their lives and as though they were not alone in their struggle. Similarly, reading about other cultures and communities around the world altered students' perception of their own circumstances, freedoms and opportunities. In a sense, students were practicing putting someone else's experience into context and exercising the power of perspective.

As has been discussed in previous findings, student abilities and confidence to express themselves as readers, writers and speakers was improving as the program year progressed – students, that is, were cultivating their voice and becoming advocates for their ideas and passions by learning how to communicating their thoughts effectively.

Students showed during book discussions and writing sessions that they had something to say, that their voice had arrived. Something that surprised us in the realm of communication, however, was the emphasis students put on their growth as listeners. In fact, listening was the most frequently selected skill on our quantitative survey asking students to identify areas of literacy skill growth after participating in the program. Students and teachers both remarked on the safe space this helped create to express opinions, digest powerful subjects within literature and share about oneself. This opened up students to make connections with each other and new groups. On this topic, students and teachers said:

"I feel like I got to know more people. I recently saw a [volunteer] at a fundraiser for our school and we started talking about [the book] and we shared our opinions. Usually I'm shy so it surprised me that we talked about the book." – student

"When I say my opinion in class, sometimes people agree or they don't, but I try to connect our opinions." – student

"Like when the volunteers came…I had already read the book, but when they came it made me see other people's opinions and consider the way other people think." – student

"What [the program provides] besides exposing them to texts, is the opportunity to discuss their opinions with communities and people who they wouldn't normally have these kinds of conversations with – like women of different races and economic status. It challenges them to articulate their passions and ideas and back them up." – teacher

Significance

Students now see themselves as part of a reading community, which has resulted in a shifted attitude towards the perspective of others and broadened world view. The ability to relate to themselves and others helps level the playing field – it's the realization that success is achievable and that they, too, can read a book, graduate high school, attend post-secondary school and start a career. Their dreams are more accessible and believable for students who have become accustomed to being marginalized. The book club has opened students' minds to their potential – showcasing that reading is a tool to not only enhance skills, but also an instrument to obtain perspective. Students have become advocates, empowered to invest in their futures and dedicated to securing their own success.

Our Response

Adjustments:

> ➤ Walk students through exercises in creating circular connections (text to self, text to someone you know, text to community, text to world).

Experiments:

> ➤ Train former Teen Services students to volunteer in the classroom as a means to mentor;
>
> ➤ Create mentor opportunities for high school students.

Finding 5: *"The World's a Book" — Attitudinal shifts about the value of reading*

A different but related shift in attitudes was around reading itself, and how it applies to one's life and the value students place on reading as an activity. In interviews, students shared the realization that reading can be anything from a magazine article, to a novel, to the Spanish captions that scroll across the television screen - recognized that reading is everywhere – intertwined in all aspects of life. One teacher noted the shift in attitude about reading from an assignment to a tool, stating:

> Since we've made inspiring the girls to relate and see themselves and their world in the text, making that the most important thing, we've gotten them to connect to reading. That psychological shift away from reading as something you have to do at school to reading as something that can help you overcome something, that reading can give you solutions to things in your life, gives a way to apply reading outside of school. Reading is a tool of liberation.

One student shared her perspective on reading and how it's changed: "I feel like I'm getting better at reading. I'm not a pro. I hated reading, now I like books, especially if they're interesting. Knowing different things, other peoples' struggles, or like relating to other peoples' stories."

Another student shared the impact reading has had in his life: "Reading gets your far, keeps you out of trouble, teaches you things you didn't know about life. I just think open, I don't think about myself, I think about my surroundings. I think about how to get further in life."

Significance

It is evident from our discussions with students participating in Adolescent Book Group, they have a better understanding of what books and reading allows them to do. They are able to better understand the world around them and become more conscientious of their surroundings. The students better understand that reading matters and is an important aspect in life because it's ubiquitous.

Our Response

Adjustments:

> Meet with classrooms one-month prior to program kick-off to encourage student participation, including facilitation, book selection, and project-based assignments.

Experiments:

> Implement problem-solving format, akin to Fieldstone Leadership;

> Recruit student ambassadors for the Words Alive/Teen Services programming.

Finding 6: *"Creating Closet Readers"* — *Challenging a stigma through ownership & access*

In line with a shift in attitudes about the value of reading, both students and teachers commented that books, book ownership and book borrowing have become more normalized among students thanks to the efforts of Adolescent Book Group. One way we do this is by encouraging students to keep any and all books they enjoyed reading in the program in order to build their home libraries (approximately seven high-quality, age-appropriate books a year). Additionally, we routinely make donations to teachers' classroom libraries to bolster student selection.

We have discussed how students come alive during book discussions with dedicated volunteers, engaged teachers and peers sharing in the safe space cultivated through the program. However, making the leap to openly projecting a commitment to reading outside the classroom is a more delicate issue for the population we serve. Almost all the students we serve are reading below grade level, and because of the adversity our students experience on a daily basis, most don't readily see themselves as good students. In fact, many students have developed a hard exterior to protect themselves and their reputations, along with a mentality that being book smart and street smart is mutual exclusive. In a way, as they are learning to value reading, they're also working to shake the myth that acquiring this new appreciation for reading lessens their credibility as a survivor on the street.

We see the in-roads forming however, sometimes in quiet ways: as one teacher commented, "to my students, it's not cool to read because of [peer] pressure. I tell them they can take the books if they want, and when I go looking for a particular book, I notice that it's missing. So I know they're taking them and reading them." Other teachers reported that students aren't "losing" their books as often or shoving them deep in their pockets before getting on the trolley. Still, other teachers shared more blatant examples: "Most of them come here hating reading, or say that they've never finished a book cover to cover. Seeing them want to take books home, or saying they want to get a certain book for someone they know, even though their barely able to put food on the table, seeing that they're passionate about a book is powerful."

And while challenging the myth of tough-kids who don't read and establishing durable reading habits takes time, by the end of the program year, more students consider reading to be an enjoyable thing to do, and that's a good place to be.

The chart on the next page depicts, on a scale of 1-5, the percent of students rating reading as a good (4) or great (5) way to spend their time.

Before and after comparison of students rating reading as a good or great way to spend time

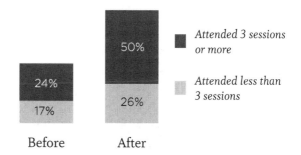

Attended 3 sessions or more

Attended less than 3 sessions

Before   After

Significance

Every day, these students combat homelessness, the stigmas of being a teen parent, incarceration, truancy or a combination of the aforementioned adversities. Although each story is different, what they have in common is that they aren't reading at grade level.

Bringing books to the classroom and providing resources to the students and teachers are ways to help raise student reading levels, sharpen their literacy skills and close the achievement gap. In 2010, The University of Nevada, Reno, published an article by Claudene Wharton about books in a home being as important as parents' education level. In the article, Wharton includes Mariah Evans' 20-year study research findings, which indicated that students who have access to books at home increases the level of education the students attain. The monthly book club, while designed to develop critical thinking skills and promote a healthy book discussion, also allows Words Alive to fill the gap for students who don't have access to books at home.

Our Response

Adjustments:

> ➤ Provide students access to read books from mobile phones;

> ➤ Connect students with the Obama eBook program that provides students at title 1 schools access to massive eBook library.

Experiments:

> ➤ Give students access to eBooks and hard copy and determine if the students who used the eBooks are more likely to finish curriculum books.

Finding 7: *"Learning together, changing together"—The power of Group Learning*

As we analyzed teacher and student interviews, we saw that group learning was driving program impact. In other words, it was the mode through which students' changing experiences with reading were coming together.

In a Momentum Learning classroom, "group learning" means student-volunteer open discussion and/or activities regarding the historical, social, economic, cultural or political issues within a selected text. An example of this in action looks like a classroom of students and a handful of volunteers, often separated in small groups, or in one large group. Trained volunteers break the ice with students by discussing whether they liked or disliked the book and then delve into the deeper, more meaningful questioning and activities. In a recent book discussion, for example, students read and discussed Speak (Laurie Halse Anderson) - a story about a teenage girl who went to a party, had a few drinks and was raped. The students, both male and female, had a great debate about who was to blame for the incident. Was it the girl's fault for dressing provocatively? Was it the boys fault for taking advantage? Was is society's fault for marketing underage drinking? These were some of the questions and points brought to the table. In the end, it resulted in a healthy debate of which students voiced their opinions and evaluated the culture to which we are exposed to. Thus, students were able to learn how to agree to disagree while establishing a shared mentality with other group members.

Across the board, teachers and students shared the behavior and attitude changes in the classroom through group learning. Although its benefits were not surprising to us, it validated our engrained program delivery:

learning as a collective. What was fascinating to discover is the evolution of the book-facilitated sessions morphing from being solely volunteer-led to being student-led. And with students at the wheel, they are now encouraged to become leaders and advocates of their own education.

Significance

Group learning is all encompassing; it connects all of the findings in that the students' communication skills towards their teachers, peers and volunteers are being developed, practiced and honed after each discussion. This is significant in allowing students who don't normally have a voice in the classroom to develop the confidence to share their thoughts and ideas. It is through the book discussion experiences where students learn to make connections through text, personally and as a group, which ignites their commitment to reading. As one teacher shared, "making [the connection between the students and the literature] is the most important thing [and Words Alive] has inspired them to make that connection to reading."

Momentum Learning is shifting their focus to deeper learning within the classroom. Most recently, this has allowed Words Alive to better develop our relationship with the San Diego Office of Education (SDCOE) and opened opportunities to work with teaching specialists and curriculum designers to select higher-level text in combination with our group learning model.

Our Response

Adjustments:

> ➢ Challenge students to focus on social justice issues, related to a book and present a solution.

Experiments:

> ➢ Implement the Tutoria concept as part of the student-led facilitation.

Conclusion

During this process we learned a deeper understanding of the value of our programs within the classrooms of which we partner. It has allowed us to see our program in a new light while igniting a passion to create a more impactful experience for our participants. Below are the Words Alive implications for our programs:

Sharpening student skillsets and supplying resources

Through our in-depth interviews with program participants and teachers, we learned that our students were not reading for comprehension. As the program continued throughout the year, teachers noted that their students began to flex skills that were sharpened through months of habitually reading, writing and discussing. Students' skillsets vary within a classroom since many of our teachers are simultaneously teaching multiple grade levels. In addition to teaching multiple grades, students have varying reading levels and skillsets. Reading is not something that comes naturally and happens through continuous practice; it is learned and looks different from culture to culture. Students cannot practice these skillsets without the necessary resources. We need to be able to provide more access to books; help increase reading levels by sharing ways to read effectively; and sharpen their basic reading skills.

Steps forward

We have a great number of volunteers who are retired teachers and principals because of the literacy focus of our organization and the work we do within schools. Some of the ways we can help our students enhance their basic reading skills include 1:1 tutoring for students reading below grade level; integrate a small-group pedagogy within the monthly book discussion to highlight vocabulary; interpretation of text and the use of evidence to support claims and ideas; and walk students through exercises in creating circular connections (text to self, text to someone you know, text to community, text to world).

We know that our students don't always have access to books. To combat this, we will provide our students opportunity to read books from their mobile phones as well as connect our students with the Obama eBook program within Title 1 classrooms, schools of which a majority of the students are living at or below poverty level, which provides entrance to a massive eBook library.

Creating student leaders

Several of our findings indicate that students learn the best when the themes, book selection and discussion sessions are student-led. In the past, we worked with our teachers and lead volunteers to select the curriculum because they know our students best. Although we ask our students to suggest books they would like to read, not all students know what their favorite book is until after participating in Words Alive. We purposely work with our teachers because they align their English Language Arts (ELA) lessons around the selected texts.

Additionally, we created a culture for our volunteers to take the lead within the book discussions. Having each volunteer facilitate one or two books per program year allowed for them to be creative during their time as facilitator in the classroom. But now is the time for us to focus on modifying our program to be led by our students; create a culture where students take responsibility of what they learn; and provide opportunities to build their confidence for necessary life-skills, such as public speaking.

Steps forward

If we plan to create student leaders, we need to build their skill-sets and allow them to take the lead in their education. We plan to do this by hosting public speaking workshops and exercises to enhance and build the student facilitation process in the classroom. We can also promote student-centric book discussion sessions by allowing students to select the theme or text for future book discussions.

We are creating student leaders by aligning the Words Alive curriculum with Thematic Interdisciplinary Project Based

Learning (TIP), Tutoria and ELA units to ensure the program is integrated into the Momentum Learning curricula. TIP is project-based learning where students create projects, like a documentary video, based upon a theme like perseverance. Students become the experts of a specific topic based on the theme and showcase what they learned through their project. Tutoria is a form of project-based learning where Student A becomes an expert in a topic and teaches Student B what they know to the point where Student B also becomes an expert.

Another alternative is to use Tutoria as our concept to implement the student-led facilitation. To do this, we would establish protocol for student facilitation, such as grade adjustment, student/volunteer preparation and define student and volunteer roles during the session.

The ELA units is a list of high-level texts created by an author hired by the San Diego County Office of Education. By using these texts in the classroom, we can ensure that we are using grade appropriate books or articles.

Strengthening the group learning environment

They say that it takes a village to raise a child. This is why our teachers, program staff, volunteers and students all have an important role in the success of our student populations. Before, almost all of our volunteers consisted of teachers and different types of school administration. As our programs grow, we will need more volunteers, some who might not have the advantage of an education background. We need to provide more training (and more in-depth training opportunities) to ensure that our volunteers are making a consistent impact across all of our classrooms.

Steps Forward

Our volunteers are the Words Alive 'word warriors' who are in the classrooms, carry-out our program. To enhance the group learning experience in the classroom, we will improve volunteer training to include methods and best practices to engage with at-risk teen populations; provide training on how to facilitate the importance of reading, interpretation and critical thinking; as well as incorporate methods to read for comprehension and annotation.

To enhance our program for the benefit of our students, Words Alive will make some programmatic changes to share with our volunteers. We plan to meet with classrooms one month prior to program kick-off to encourage student participation, including facilitation, book selection and project-based assignments; as well as implement a mid-month check-in prior to the book discussion and writing program to encourage more participation amongst students.

From our findings, we found that group learning was driving our program impact in the classroom. Through our discussions with our teaching specialists at the San Diego County Office of Education (SDCOE), we learned that even though our students are not reading at grade-level, if the books are high-level and interesting, the group learning environment is perfect setting to dissect a novel. Moving forward, we plan to challenge our students to work on social justice issues related to a book and present a solution; create more sharing opportunities of their writing and project-based assignments for our students to showcase their solutions; implement expository writing within monthly writing program sessions and/or book club discussions.

Just in Time for Foster Youth

Pathways to Financial Power

Don Wells
Executive Director

Allison Bechill
Associate Director

Trish Horton
Volunteer Engagement Manager

Vanessa Davis
Youth Services Lead Coordinator

Marquelle Edwards
Youth Services Lead Coordinator

Introduction

Just in Time for Foster Youth (JIT) engages a caring community to help transitioning foster youth achieve self-sufficiency and well being. We envision a future in which every young person leaving foster care has a community of caring adults waiting for them after 18. We believe disconnection is the major obstacle they face so consistent, long-term relationship-based services becomes the foundation for the success and durable change so they can thrive and enjoy productive, satisfying lives.

Every effective parent knows the lasting impact they want to have on their children's lives requires time, personal attention, individual and customized guidance, repetition, genuine interest in their well being, and a broad range of experiences and connections that give them the opportunity to grow by both failing and succeeding.

The challenges faced by every young adult are compounded for youth leaving foster care. Having suffered trauma when removed from their biological home, they become increasingly disconnected as they move from one placement to another.

Without a supportive community, transitioning foster youth are at risk of being homeless, unemployed, and under-educated. Challenged by limited access to consistent education, employment opportunities, and independence-building stepping stones such as learning to manage money or to drive, the biggest gap they must overcome is the shattered ability to establish meaningful connections.

JIT mobilizes community volunteers as an extended family for transitioning foster youth through cultivated relationships and emergency resources provided by individuals, agencies, businesses and foundations that share our core values and mission.

JIT currently offers multiple services that focus on providing consistent support to transitioning foster youth to help them on their path to self-sufficiency in the areas of stable housing, essential education, meaningful employment, financial security, reliable transportation, positive connections, confidence and well-being.

In fiscal year 2016, JIT staff and nearly 600 community volunteers served over 850 youth through one or more of our services.

Critical Features of JIT Services and Theory of Change

To further our mission, JIT anticipates serving approximately 900 unduplicated transitioning foster youth from July 2016-June 2017 and 1,000-1,200 in July 2017-June 2018 through distributions and connections across multiple services to move the needle significantly on JIT's Self-Sufficiency & Well Being Scale.

Ultimately, our unique approach to youth-centered, relationship-based services are built upon a powerful theory of change based on individual empowerment, earned trust, and consistent response to youth need. Specifically, our support of youth has the following critical features:

1. We engage youth in consistent relationships with volunteers whenever possible

2. We employ former foster youth as staff in service delivery and other leadership roles

3. We stress authentic relationships in all youth contacts

4. We stress individualized approaches to all services, with participants as our collaborative partners

5. We focus on all aspects of youth needs, not only the presenting issue

6. We respond proactively to needs as they arise, both for the individual and the population as a whole

7. We constantly evolve our services by keeping our "finger on the pulse" of youth need

This approach is rooted in the following principles:

➤ A life of Uncertainty and Disconnection is the core obstacle for transitioning foster youth, therefore **consistent connection** is the core solution.

➤ There is tremendous power in **seeing yourself in the person you reach out to** when you must share your story and be vulnerable. And more power in being able to see your possible success in theirs.

➤ Without **real trust**, there can be no lasting transformative connection.

➤ Every youth is **unique**.

➤ Every youth has the power to **create their own success**.

➤ Well being is only possible with a **holistic understanding** of what is truly needed.

➤ **Timely intervention at a critical juncture** is the difference between hope and despair.

➤ Meeting the dynamically changing needs of youth requires **curiosity, creativity and courage.**

Pathways to Financial Power

Given the tenuous financial situation transitioning foster youth face, it is essential to help build structures in their lives that can buffer them against inevitable setbacks and emergencies. Helping youth develop and take advantage of greater earning power and supporting them through the process of obtaining good first jobs is a priority foundation for the self-sufficiency and well-being we seek.

Pathways to Financial Power creates a platform to generate support for JIT's commitment to mobilize the community to help transitioning foster youth achieve self-sufficiency and well-being through smart money management, access to connections, and opportunities for meaningful employment - all provided by individuals and organizations that can assist young men and women to reach that goal.

The long term impact for our community is that foster youth and public perceptions change from the inevitability of negative foster care outcomes to increased hope, resources and direct community support for this population. The resulting change in expectations when this relationship-based model is used means the cycle of foster care is broken for all transitioning youth and their children who remain out of the system.

Intended Impact

Pathways to Financial Power brings together all of Just in Time's services in a multi-year, individualized and comprehensive approach that mirrors what a healthy family provides its children. It connects transitioning youth to community-based resources for smart money management, capacity building to apply for a job, and opportunities for meaningful employment, provided by individuals and partnering organizations.

The effort launched in 2015 with the Pathways to Financial Power Conference and a cohort of 65 young men and women motivated to pursue a better paying job and the desire to build a stronger financial foundation. After assessing each participant's career goals and employment readiness, JIT helped remove obstacles to securing jobs at a living wage. This includes mandatory workshops on resume building, interview skills and creating a written roadmap to desired outcomes. The Pathways Conference introduces participants to more interactive workshops; capacity building resources that address existing challenges or create new opportunities for progress in affordable housing, reliable transportation and access to education/ training; and ready-to-hire employers offering meaningful jobs connected to career goals.

Specifically, there are three key intended impact goals for Pathways participants that were addressed in both the quantitative and quality data gathered. These are:

Transitioning foster youth achieve financial security. By this we mean youth are able to: define and are invested in their own self-sufficiency and path to success; attain the evolving education needed to support their aspirations; develop translatable skill sets; learn and use the most effective methods to acquire meaningful employment; build the knowledge to access essential resources and confidently navigate the workplace; and learn and practice effective financial management, including budgeting, savings and establishing strong credit.

Transitioning foster youth develop and leverage supportive relationships. By this we mean youth have a strong understanding of the essential importance of relationships and connections to achieving their personal and professional success and well-being; establish, grow and leverage a network of relationships in order to thrive; and seek out and flourish in interdependent communities that empower them to accept themselves, embrace support, and have the satisfaction of giving back to others.

Transitioning foster youth define themselves, their power and their future. By this we mean youth have awareness of their strengths and put them to work to overcome obstacles and advance their goals; are consistently proactive rather than reactive; demonstrate the personal confidence and resiliency to successfully navigate life's challenges, setbacks and opportunities; develop their personal authentic voice to share their own stories and become effective advocates for themselves and others; and establish positive personal habits—physical, mental, emotional—that contribute to long term, sustainable health.

Evaluation Methodology

The purpose of our evaluation was to explore the scope and quality of our intended impact on a population of transitioning foster youth based on their specific experience with services related to the goals of Pathways to Financial Power. This included workshops targeting employment obstacles prior to the September Pathways Conference, participation in JIT services that encouraged networking and soft skills, attendance at the Conference itself, and follow-up participation in the JIT community for six months after the Conference. During this period, we (a) developed and refined our ideas of intended impact and indicators, (b) designed and implemented both qualitative and quantitative means to collect and analyze data, and (c) identified findings and considered the implications to those findings for program adjustments and additions.

This evaluative process began with a focus on identifying and clarifying the intended impact of Pathways to Financial Power since it best represented the holistic nature of JIT's approach to durable change. Once the ideas had been developed, and indicators identified, we designed interview protocol to collect qualitative data from a representative sample of Pathways participants and a questionnaire to track quantitative measures for a complete picture of our results. These data were analyzed, themes identified, and then translated into findings. From the findings, we developed useful service insights and enhancements that will have ramifications throughout the organization.

Qualitative Data and Analysis

Our qualitative approach followed these steps:

1. **Protocol Design.** We designed an in-depth interview protocol using the Heart Triangle method of question construction. This produced a protocol consisting of ten sequences of questions (38 questions in total). The protocol was our guide to collect data about the subjects' awareness and reflection of structural shifts and developments of growth and progress.

2. **Sample.** We identified a sample of subjects using a purposeful stratified technique to select a representation of the population we served. Our population size was 65. Our sample size was 22 and we drew our sample from the following strata of our population: Transitioning foster youth 18-26, 66% female, 34% male.

3. **Data Collection.** We convened one-on-one Interviews lasting from 45 minutes to one hour in length. Data were collected via notes during the interview, and then augmented immediately following the interview to provide a substantive rendering of the interview.

4. **Data Analysis.** We applied a four-step model of textual analysis to each of the interviews. This process allowed us to interpret the meaning Themes. We then examined the overarching themes that emerged from the full scope of our data analysis to illuminate the primary insights and discoveries.

Quantitative Data and Analysis

We also designed a questionnaire to collect data on our quantitative indicators of impact. We administered this instrument to 22 Pathways youth participants. The data were analyzed primarily using measures of central tendency.

Findings

In our interviews, participants spoke about being exposed to knowledge and experiences that led to a more expanded and expressive view of life, increasing their credibility and ability to solve the problems at hand. They talked about learning self-awareness, their value, and understanding their place in the world because they now realize they are no different than "successful" people. Participants also gained the power of owning and sharing their own stories and converting a painful past into a source of empathy, proactivity and confidence. They also describe the foundational importance of authentic, mutually supportive relationships in helping them set healthy personal and professional boundaries and make lasting connections based on consistency and trust. These four outcomes created a mutually reinforcing "tipping point" in deep, durable change in self-perception and personal empowerment.

Finding #1: *Mind the GAP (What's Tripping You Up?)*

For many foster youth, moving from home to home before the age of 18 has disrupted their schooling and created gaps in their knowledge. While it's easy to imagine how switching teachers mid-year would disrupt a young person's learning of mathematics or English, it's less common to notice the gap in life skills and experiences that hold former foster youth back. JIT develops programs and services to help close these gaps for young adults 18-26 who are transitioning out of the foster care system.

Pathways to Financial Power delivers a unique mix of experiences and skill-building that meets each young adult where they are in life. In our interviews with participants, it was apparent that specific knowledge gained through JIT programs —along with personal and professional experiences shared with volunteers—work cumulatively over time to create transformative change. Knowledge such as how to set up a savings account and deposit a portion of every paycheck into it; how to develop and use a budget while also taking steps to establish strong credit (Fig 1a); and learning the ins and outs of networking and interviewing, then putting those skills and tools into practice with JIT volunteers.

Fig. 1a: Using a Budget, Adding to Savings, Knowing Credit Score

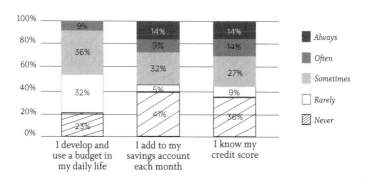

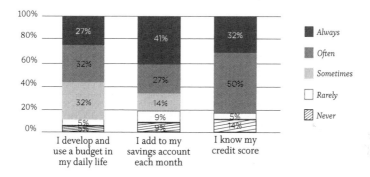

Different JIT participants have different gaps in life skills and experiences – and whatever is "tripping them up" at a given time is different for each of them. That's why our programs and services include a community of caring adults who provide guidance and emotional support. These volunteers' consistent presence is critical to filling gaps that only people can; such as being the role model for how to dress professionally, something that was missing for many participants while growing up. Or the volunteer that supports a youth to "speak my truth and say what I feel, and not let someone else's voice overshadow mine."

One participant described the building blocks that led her to ask for a raise and receive a significant promotion at work after recognizing her value while networking with an employer at a Pathways event; building a stronger resume and her confidence during the Career Horizons program; and talking with her Financial Fitness asset advisor about being underpaid for the quality and quantity of work she produced at her job. Over nine months, new experiences and new knowledge compounded as she gained confidence and formed new connections with people. She practiced negotiating for that promotion and also talked with a volunteer life coach about ways her reliance on "Command," discovered through a StrengthsFinder assessment, was getting in the way at work. The different people and programs she was introduced to in the JIT community filled the gaps she previously had in knowledge, relationships, and experience.

The Pathways process makes programs, relationships, and experiences available to youth when they need them. By giving these connected young adults the power of choice over what they participate in and when, it helps them become more confident because they feel more capable with the knowledge they have acquired (Fig 1b).

One participant credits the Career Horizons program with helping her overcome her shyness, make connections with amazing women, and develop her confidence to the point where she said "Now I know I can do it. I'm pretty much achieving everything I put my mind to." She continued, "Before I had a hard time building relationships. Because I was abandoned as a child I thought 'Why build connections if you never know they will be there' But now I know I can build relationships and I'm not alone; I have a group of people I can call on when I need support."

Fig. 1b: Creating Goals, Using LinkedIn, Establishing Credit

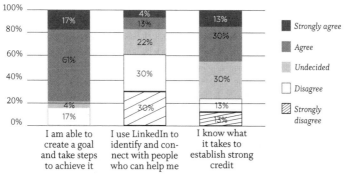

Before Pathways

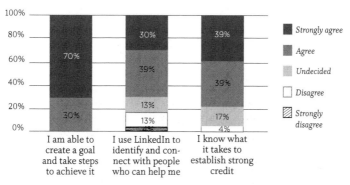

After Pathways

Significance

Most transitioning foster youth have not had a family to fall back on or support their dreams and aspirations. The Pathways initiative empowers these young people by providing programs, services, and a community of volunteers that help them close gaps in knowledge and life experience.

Pathways connects youth participants with programs like Bridges to Success for Young Men, Career Horizons for Young Women, Financial Fitness, My First Home, and Healthy Practices. It exposes them to new experiences like life coaching, Pilates, behind-the-wheel driving practice, culinary training, and surfing.

One participant explained how JIT has filled different gaps for her at different points in time; she says she was never lost and always knew what direction she wanted to go but needed the support a family would usually provide. When it came time for her to take the LSAT in preparation to apply to law school, she still had a gap in knowledge and test-taking skills so JIT stepped in, paying for the Kaplan prep course she needed to prepare for and ultimately pass the exam. Another participant shared that she attended every Financial Fitness workshop when she was enrolled in that program and, by applying what she learned, she saved $4000. This gave her the power to visit her biological parents in Mexico. She had not seen them for 14 years and needed to understand their actions where she was concerned. It was the right decision for her, she says, providing the closure she wanted. And, after making the trip she still has $2000 in savings. Pathways empowers young people to gain new knowledge and life experiences that would otherwise be out of their reach.

Possible Recommendations

➤ Identify individual knowledge/experience gaps during initial assessment and regular follow up

➤ Determine optimal timing on access to opportunities and exposure to enhancing experiences

Findings # 2: *Pathway from "Failure" to "Fabulous"*

Self-awareness is to truly know one's self or to realize the truth of one's existence. However, for former foster youth a sense of self can be shrouded with negative feelings of inferiority and inadequacy. Popular notions of former foster youth label them as delinquents, criminals, and burdens to society. Many foster youth learn of these stereotypes at a very young age and this negative thinking follows them into adulthood and becomes their identity.

JIT's Pathways to Financial Power Initiative introduced transitioning foster youth to JIT's services which have helped them identify self-limiting beliefs, develop self-awareness, and understand and leverage their strengths. During our interviews we consistently heard from Pathways participants that they now know their place in the world, have more control over their life, and enjoy a greater sense of self-awareness that caused a shift in the emotional quality of their relationships. Through their involvement in services first introduced during their participation in Pathways - such as one-on-one mentorship with career coaches and participation in Strength Finders Workshops - participants also report feeling empowered in their personal and professional life. Focusing on and learning about their strengths has also allowed them to be more confident and accepting of weaknesses (Fig 2a). In our survey, confidence levels increased dramatically from 41% reporting "a lot" or "quite a bit" of confidence to nearly double that amount at 77%. Those who responded with "a little" or "none" to the confidence question dropped from 28% to 9% after Pathways.

Fig. 2a: Confidence about Interviewing

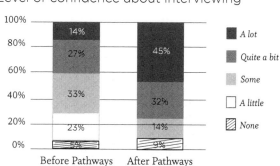

Level of confidence about interviewing

As a result of Pathways, participants are provided with the skills needed to advocate within their own lives, recognize and embrace their strengths, and change self-limiting beliefs. And they express that change in powerful ways:

"I have always felt that I wasn't good enough. I had a chip on my shoulder. I am beginning to see that I matter and I'm not a failure. This has helped me in my relationships with people because I feel like I am no longer being judged as a failure."

"When I think negative thoughts about myself, I am able to recognize that those thoughts are not my reality that I am a good person and people care about me. It has taken a lot of work but I like who I am as a person the good, the bad and the ugly. I am not scared of making mistakes or failing anymore."

"When someone asks me what I am good at nowadays, I can answer confidently! I used to dread that question during interviews but I wait for it now. I list my strengths and I have examples of how I have used those strengths in the past, this has been my biggest takeaway."

Despite the growth in positive empowerment, our surveys also showed that Pathways was most effective in reducing anxiety about networking with youth who initially only had "some" anxiety but the experience had relatively little effect on those reporting "quite a bit" or "a lot of anxiety" before Pathways (Fig 2b). This would indicate that those with higher levels of anxiety should be identified as quickly so that additional measures can be taken to assist them.

Fig. 2b: Anxiety about Networking

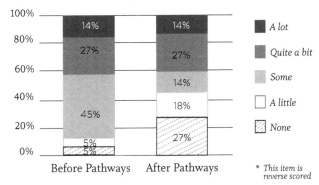

Before Pathways   After Pathways

* This item is reverse scored

Significance

It was enlightening to hear during our interviews that so many participants reported experiencing a transformative change and increase in confidence from their participation in taking the StrengthsFinders assessment and attending workshops that helped them learn more about their strengths. As a result of this finding, JIT has invested in having a greater amount of participants take the assessment and go through training to learn about strengths.

Possible Recommendations

➤ Identify "high anxiety" youth and offer enhanced tools

➤ Use StrengthsFinder assessments more pervasively, outside of current cohort services

➤ Stagger expansion through targeted approach

➤ Incorporate self-limiting beliefs and strengths concepts in more workshops

➤ Develop more formal Peer-to-Peer relationship/coaching

➤ Offer more individual coaching as needed

➤ Incorporate EMDR-type services for trauma reduction

Finding #3: *Put It On Loudspeaker!*

For many former foster youth, their past is a source of shame—something to hide, repress, or even fear. They are rightfully eager to leave painful experiences behind them, and to create an identity free from the label of "foster child," and all the assumptions and judgments that so often accompany it.

One aspect of JIT's Pathways to Financial Power initiative is to provide participants the tools they need to not only craft a confident elevator pitch and sell themselves to potential employers, but also to shift their own perception of their story. To transform it from a source of shame to a point of pride. To see it not as a weakness, but as a source of strength—an inspiration for others.

Fig. 3: Since Pathways, I can more confidently share my story.

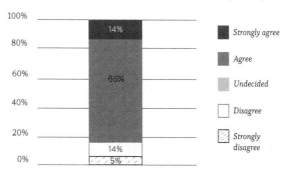

"I'm still learning how to represent myself," noted one participant. "I used to try to put the past in the past. Just in Time helped me own my identity and use it for good rather than being fearful of it." She went on to explain that owning her story increased her own sense of self-worth, as well as her empathy for others. "Embracing where I come from made me more understanding of where others come from...it made me want to say to them that if I can do it, so can they."

Another participant added that the public speaking and storytelling training she received through JIT helped her, in her words, to recognize her own accomplishments. "I loved speaking," she said, obviously still surprised by this revelation months after the experience. "[Sharing my story] was like a weight lifted off my shoulders." She went on to say that, after speaking at a JIT event, she is no longer ashamed about her story. She said that she found the experience motivating, one that made her want to do more of it. Through the experience, she realized that people responded to her story with empathy, not judgment. She was also inspired hearing the stories of her peers at the Pathways to Financial Power conference.

Significance

Storytelling has always been an integral part of JIT's DNA. Yet we were still surprised by the transformative, positive change that our interviewees credited to their experience with owning and sharing their stories. This finding has encouraged us to provide storytelling training and opportunities for public speaking to more JIT participants beyond Pathways to Financial Power.

Possible Recommendations

> Provide more Intentional storytelling training

> Create tiers/stages of storytelling development—elevator speech to public speaking

> Establish JIT "Toastmasters" and/or Speakers Bureau

> Institute "train the trainers resource"

➤ Develop capacity in other storytelling modes—written, video, art

Finding #4: *Wrapped in Relationships*

Connecting the population we serve to a caring community has always been at the forefront of our services. We have found that amongst the many services we provide, establishing meaningful relationships is most important for sustainable self-sufficiency. For many former foster youth, this proves to be an overwhelmingly difficult task. It contradicts the survival lessons life in the foster care system has taught them. It encourages them to be vulnerable, and in their world, vulnerability has always been viewed as a weakness. When betrayal has been quintessentially imbedded in their interactions with adults, this hinders their ability and willingness to trust again. Part of the Pathways to Financial Power initiative is to provide participants the platform required to not only initiate a long lasting connection with volunteers within the community, but to also sharpen their networking skills with potential employers.

Through Pathways to Financial Power workshops, participants are made aware of behaviors that may be affecting their personal relationships and professional opportunities. Also, through these workshops, participants are learning how paramount social networking tools, such as Facebook and LinkedIn, are in making and keeping connections. Of Pathways participants surveyed:

➤ 100% of youth have developed 1 or more personal contacts.

➤ 91% have deepened relationships and established a greater level of trust with 1 or more of their existing contacts

➤ 68% have a new career/job-related contact

Participants shared the unexpected sense of relief they discovered once connections were made.

"I've have never felt anyone had my best interest at heart. I always thought I had to do everything on my own. Being part of JIT and

Pathways to Financial Power, I know I'm not alone. I know that if I make a mistake in life, I will not be judged by it. I'm able to fall and receive help to stand up again."

"JIT and Pathways to Financial Power helped me to believe in people again. I'm able to talk to someone before I make decisions. I'm so happy I don't always have to learn things the hard way. I have met people that I know will be in my life forever and that feels so good."

"Everything from Pathways was genuine. People really wanted to get to know me. In the beginning it was weird for me. I didn't think it was real. I thought, 'here we go again.' It wasn't until after the event was over I realized how sincere people were. I received calls to check on me just to see if I was ok. Then I was invited to lunches just to check in. That's when I really opened up. I shared some personal stories and the volunteer did the same. I was also helped out with some homework. I'm happy I was able to connect with someone that I can depend on."

Pathways to Financial Power highlights participant's hesitation to establish connections after a life of negative personal experiences. It also demonstrates that, if presented with an opportunity, these young adults are eager and willing be part of mutually rewarding relationships.

Significance

Connections are the cornerstone of all services. Hearing the impact these connections have had on the interviewees has reinforced what we already know to be true. This finding has encouraged us to provide more opportunities for youth and volunteers to build mutual rapport. We plan to incorporate more opportunities to deepen participant to volunteer connections. Also, we want to ensure that our participants have multiple long lasting and meaningful relationships. This will continue to strengthen our already effective model.

Possible Recommendations

- ➢ Create digital Community of Support (social media groups)
- ➢ Hold a Mid-year Reunion
- ➢ Create Peer Focused communities
- ➢ Use a Volunteer Team approach
- ➢ Encourage the use of Connection Cards for peers at events and the elevate the possibility of connections for "transactional" services

Finding #5: *Tipping Points: Sparking an Epidemic of Positive Self-Perception for Transitioning Foster Youth*

In his book *"Tipping Point"*, Malcolm Gladwell describes how ideas, trends and cultural changes spread rapidly when three essential agents intersect: "infectious" people, "sticky" content, and a "contagious" environment. In their interviews with Just in Time for Foster Youth staff, transitioning foster youth who participated in Pathways to Financial Power consistently mentioned four interconnected core factors that sparked transformative growth in their positive self-perception and coincide with Gladwell's paradigm.

In concept, Pathways is designed to select youth with an expressed commitment to achieving financial security but who still lack the confidence, capacity and connections to do so, then exposes them to multiple JIT services in an environment that maximizes the benefits of each one. Pathways participants interviewed said that not only have gaps in their knowledge of financial management and access to meaningful employment been filled, but they also furthered engagement with "sticky" JIT services that helped identify self-limiting beliefs and real personal strengths; gained more ownership of their personal stories and discovered their "infectious" voice; and made new "contagious" connections to trusted relationships with supportive adults and a network of positive peers.

Specifically, participants spoke about being exposed to knowledge and experiences that led to a more expanded and expressive view of life, increasing their credibility and ability to solve the problems at hand. They talked about learning self-awareness, their value, and understanding their place in the world because they now realize they are no different than "successful" people. Participants also gained the power of owning and sharing their own stories and converting a painful past into a source of empathy, proactivity and confidence. And they described the foundational importance of authentic, mutually supportive relationships in helping them set healthy personal and professional boundaries and make lasting connections based on consistency and trust. These four outcomes created a mutually reinforcing "tipping point" in deep, durable change in self-perception and personal empowerment.

One participant shared how her self-perception has changed:

> I'm not trying to fill anyone else's shoes anymore. For foster youth, it's particularly hard not to try being someone else because you don't like being who you were. The need to change shows up in life almost every day and takes a continuous shift in perspective. It's constant work, like watering a plant, but now I have no fear of "sitting at the table" with anyone.

Another participant, when asked about feeling valued, said:

> My own perception was influenced by expanding my network and talking to people. At Pathways I learned about the need for engineers in the job market. This made me realize there is value in being an engineer, doing the work, and doing it well. Before, I used to think "I'm just an engineer". Now, "I'm an electrical engineer at a medical device company." Also, now I trust myself to know the answers and not worry what others think of me. Otherwise, it's like allowing someone to go in your house and redecorate.

Significance

This finding highlights four core drivers of transformative change in self-perception and empowerment for transitioning foster that have implications for JIT's increased emphasis on services that most clearly support exposure to the powerful, demonstrable benefits described. They also point to the cumulative effect of those drivers; the idea that a youth's concurrent involvement with all four factors is mutually reinforcing and creates a "tipping point" in increased optimism, self-advocacy and mastery. The findings will help determine JIT's allocation of resources to strengthen elements that most clearly drive our intended impact, require us to extend those elements to youth who historically are outside of services that most strongly focus on the core dimensions identified, and ensure that we engage as many youth as possible in ways that include all four dimensions as quickly as possible.

Possible Recommendations

➤ Consistent tracking of all JIT youth for 4 drivers from onboarding to exit at 26

Steps Forward: Priority Recommendations to Expand Support for Durable Change

These five powerful findings provide a clear path for broadening, deepening and reinforcing JIT's impact though this specific service and enhancing our lasting change in ways that are consistent with and further the implementation of Theory of Change. Specifically, we have identified these priority recommendations as our focus over the next 12 months.

I. Fill Gaps in Knowledge/Experience

Initial assessment with new participants *(immediately)*

This initial assessment could be done through the Pathways application and the Pathways plan, with individualized benchmarks for structured follow up (weekly or biweekly from pre-conference activities through the conference and monthly at a minimum thereafter). Each Pathways participant will be assigned to a dedicated staff member.

The initial assessment will take place in August and September of each year, as a new group of Pathways participants begin their pre-conference work. The first three priorities for this Step Forward are to

1. identify which a la carte services will be offered and when

2. create the assessment questions/scoring

3. develop the delivery model (including volunteers)

Follow-up intervals will be specific to the selected services (i.e. monthly peer group check-ins on job search, quarterly volunteer-youth workshops on applying StrengthsFinder to daily life, 6-month checkups with a YS staff member).

Regular follow up with current participants *(immediately - staggered by service)*

Our qualitative interviews revealed there is a cumulative effect as youth participate in additional programs and services - and those who participate in JIT's cohort programs experience even more benefits. The knowledge and experience they gain are relevant for each youth at different times, a function of who they are as individuals and what life circumstances arise. This led us to a new model that makes the most popular aspects of each cohort program accessible to all youth in an a la carte way.

Pathways participants would be guided to self-assess regularly, building and refining their own unique plan by selecting skills-building opportunities with specific timelines. They would be empowered to identify and prioritize what they need and when, since durable change develops over a long period of time and is different for each youth. Because volunteer and peer relationships are integral to participants' success and well-being, we plan to facilitate more pairings between youth and volunteers - and more small group work - more often. In this way we'll bring interpersonal support and a sense of community to more transitioning foster youth, enlarging their circle of support.

Timing on access opportunities/exposure *(beginning July 2016)*

We will begin by rolling out the most needed and useful opportunities first. (i.e. resume preparation, mock interviewing, the job search, networking, goal-setting, budgeting, and saving.) We'll work with our new corporate partners to build an annual plan that helps youth close their gaps in skills and experience, with volunteer and peer support along the way. There would be pre-conference workshops and prep work, then quarterly opportunities to join a certain service track.

> ➤ Example: Corporate staffing agency Apple One (AO) holds a group resume writing workshop and later a social media branding workshop, AO volunteers work one-on-one with youth to finalize their resumes, AO volunteers work one-on-one with youth to create a job search plan and connect them with job openings, we add in JIT social mixers for AO volunteers to deepen their relationships with these youth).

> ➤ Example: Mission Federal Bank hosts a series of financial literacy workshops on topics such as budgeting. Youth participants get a special match when opening a savings account at Mission Fed. Youth build relationships with local branch managers who offer in-person guidance on financial matters.

II. From Self-limiting Beliefs to Maximizing Strengths

Identify High Anxiety participants and create anxiety reducing resources in Pathways *(summer 2017)*

JIT will reach out to participants from the 2015 cohort to identify high anxiety participants based on interviews and responses to quantitative questionnaire and also identifying participants of Pathways 2016 that have high anxiety. They will be invited to Healthy Practices workshops focused on dealing with anxiety and encouraged to take advantage of one on one coaching and engage in networking practice through JIT events. This will be an ongoing process beginning August 2016.

Pervasive use of StrengthsFinder *(staggered expansion through services in the next 6 months)*

This rollout will differ depending on the program. It has already been implemented in all cohort services, except Financial Fitness. It will be offered to Financial Fitness participants and non-cohort youth through scheduled workshops by January 2017.

StrengthsFinders could also be done as part of the onboarding process for new participants (perhaps once they've demonstrated commitment through a to-be-determined amount of engagement activities (workshops, coaching sessions, etc.) This also will be explored for implementation by January 2017.

Individual Coaching *(immediately)*

This has been an ongoing service currently provided to all of JIT participants. Youth Services and Volunteer engagement will work to increase the number of youth being offered this service.

Peer-to-Peer relationship/coaching *(summer 2016)*

During Pathways 2016, JIT recruit Pathways alumni to develop smaller accountability groups to act as role models, support and peer-to-peer mentors.

EMDR-type Services *(beginning August 2016)*

EMDR (Eye Movement Desensitization and Reprocessing) is a fairly new type of psychotherapy that is growing in popularity, particularly for treating post-traumatic stress disorder (PTSD). JIT will explore the effective use of EMDR for our participants beginning with a staff/youth group in August 2016 and then expand the service to be available to all participants if deemed appropriate.

III. Authentic Voices and Owning Their Stories

Intentional storytelling training *(beginning Fall 2016)*

This will be accomplished through a workshop facilitated by Karen Dietz before, during, and following the conference. Other resources (such as Launchbox) might also be used depending on available financial resources. Depending on resources, these could also be opened up to other JIT participants.

JIT "Toastmasters" and/or Speakers Bureau *(complete by spring 2017)*

This initiative will be incorporated into the goals of the incoming Brand, Communications and Marketing Coordinator's goals as outlined on his/her Performance scorecard. One goal of the Intentional Storytelling Training (above) would be to identify the most promising potential speakers and offer them the opportunity to progress to participating in the Speakers Bureau, where they would receive a higher level of training and the opportunity to represent JIT at speaking engagements, where they would receive a stipend.

IV. Supportive Relationships

Connection Cards for Peers at events & for "transactional" services *(immediately)*

Connection Cards will be provided at the Pathways orientation, at prep-sessions prior to the Conferences and at every Pathways gathering. Strategies on how to maximize the functionality of the cards will be communicated at every JIT service opportunity or event, including through social media success stories.

Community of Support through social media groups *(beginning Fall 2016)*

This initiative will also be incorporated into the goals of the incoming Brand, Communications and Marketing Coordinator's goals as outlined on his/her Performance scorecard in collaboration with a Youth Services Coordinator who monitor the groups and reply to youth as appropriate. LEAP members could also be tapped to moderate these groups.

The Social media groups would be used with "connection cards", before and after the Pathways event. If used properly, a Facebook group would be created prior to the event once the youth and volunteers have been selected. It would be used as a message board and to generate some awareness and excitement. A weekly update weekly by Pathways Alumni or Volunteers with a "did you know" post would highlight resources, success stories and opportunities before, during and after the conference creating an ongoing community of success.

Mid-year Reunion *(February or April 2017)*

We will host a reunion to bring Pathways participants together to support ongoing relationship-building.

V. Tipping Points

Track all youth for 4 drivers from onboarding to age 26
(6 months to full implementation)

This should be addressed and accomplished via our Salesforce overhaul in process being July 2016. We will determine the best way to track this data, such as program participation, distributions, etc. We may need to develop a quarterly survey that is deployed through Salesforce (or deployed through a system that can automatically populate their Salesforce profile). Youth Services staff will have accurate tracking and regular youth reports on progress as part of their performance measures.

Olivewood Gardens and Learning Center

Cooking for Salud™

Cherianne Barry
Nutrition Program Coordinator

Diana Bergman
Program Director

Claire Groebner
Development Assistant

Acknowledgements

We would like to express our profound gratitude to the Olivewood Kitchenistas who graciously shared their experiences, struggles, and personal journeys with us throughout the data collection process. We are inspired and honored by their commi™ents to their families, community, and health. We would also like to acknowledge Clara Estrella-Varela and Esperanza Guerrero for volunteering their time to support this meticulous process. Our analysis of this program would not have been possible without their dedication to this project.

Thank you to Steve Patty and Jessamyn Luiz from Dialogues in Action for challenging us to reflect deeply about our work and the process of evaluation. Your thoughtful guidance will help improve our organizational efforts of building healthier families and a healthier environment.

We would also like to thank The Gumpert Foundation for believing in the programs and the potential of Olivewood Gardens and Learning Center, and for providing us with this invaluable professional development opportunity.

Lastly, we would like to acknowledge Kati Christensen, the Olivewood Gardens Chef Educator who founded the program in 2013. Thanks to Kati for starting a program that is changing lives!

Executive Summary

Olivewood Gardens and Learning Center's Cooking for Salud™ parent nutrition education program is designed to teach parents how to make healthy changes at home that will improve their families' short and long-term health outcomes. Created to address the diet-related disease crisis occurring in our community, Cooking for Salud™ is a behavior modification program that gives families tools to change their cooking and eating habits, as well as transform the way they view food and health. Over the past four years, the program has graduated seven generations of "Kitchenistas" that have gone on to participate in Resident Leadership Academies, community outreach, and volunteerism with Olivewood.

Program Goals:

Goal #1: Kitchenistas mindfully prepare and consume food.

Goal #2: Families are engaged in healthy eating decisions and practices.

Goal #3: Kitchenistas are ambassadors of healthy eating in their family and community.

To assess the success of our program in meeting these goals, we performed in-depth, in person interviews with Kitchenistas (program graduates) from the most recent three generations to capture qualitative data. To collect quantitative results, we created and administered a survey that was disseminated to all graduates of the program. Key findings include:

➢ **"If at first you don't succeed, pick yourself up and try again"**: Graduates of Cooking for Salud™ demonstrated the importance of resiliency in making changes around food. Through the lessons and support they received from Cooking for Salud™, participants felt that they were able to overcome obstacles and resistance from family, recognizing that change takes time and perseverance.

➢ **It worked:** Participants did in fact change their eating habits as a result of what they learned in Cooking for Salud™. Given tools and practice making healthy substitutions, increasing the use of vegetables and fruits in meals, and reading labels, participants were able to make changes in their personal lives to support health.

➢ **Mi salud es su salud:** Graduates of the program overwhelmingly reported a shift in their thinking about health and community. By connecting with other women with similar struggles and backgrounds and being a part of an organization meant to serve the community, participants took ownership over their health, their families' health, and the health of their community, recognizing that all are connected. The majority of graduates report feeling confident sharing about health in their community.

In addition to these findings, our research demonstrated that graduates find health to be an important goal and driving factor in their decision-making, and that food, meal preparation, and sharing are important cultural factors that are integral to a sense of purpose and satisfaction in life. Cooking for Salud™ provided participants not only with tools for changing eating habits, but a space in which to explore new ways of imagining traditions. Through our data analysis, we also discovered ways to improve on the successes of the Cooking for Salud™ program, including limiting the program participants to residents of our local community, creating a family day to engage participants' children and spouses in healthy meal preparation, and including time, structure, and support for participants to discuss obstacles and ways to overcome them.

Who We Are

Olivewood Gardens and Learning Center empowers students and families from diverse backgrounds to be healthy and active citizens through organic gardening, environmental stewardship, and nutrition education. Our center is located in the heart of National City, California. Donated in 2006 by Christy Walton, this beautiful 6.85-acre property includes a historic home, extensive organic vegetable gardens, greenhouse, chickens, fruit trees, worm bin, year-round flowers, and a view of the ocean. Our team includes credentialed teachers, agriculture experts, and over 350 volunteers. Our purpose is to build healthy families and a healthy environment.

Founded in 2008 by the International Community Foundation, Olivewood Gardens and Learning Center was established to provide access to organic gardens for low income school children. The first field trips for students began in 2010. In 2013, Olivewood hosted the first Cooking for Salud™ series as a response to the community's need for adult nutrition education. We are now a dynamic, engaging organization that is the result of philanthropy, San Diego's food movement, and local neighborhoods coming together to address nutrition and health issues in the border region.

Today, Olivewood Gardens provides hands-on and standards-based gardening, science, and nutrition education for children and adults. Learning is centered within the context of our organic gardens and a demonstration kitchen. The seasons dictate the food prepared in the kitchen, and the rhythm of activity within the garden.

Description of Program

Cooking for Salud™ is a 7-week bilingual series of classes focused on teaching parents to create a healthy kitchen within their own homes. Cooking for Salud™ is designed to increase the confidence of the participants, affectionately known as Kitchenistas, so that they can change their daily eating habits and prepare healthy meals for themselves and their families. With the expertise and guidance of volunteers, including local chefs and community partners, the Kitchenistas explore techniques for preparing flavorful vegetables, healthy salad dressings and sauces, whole grains, lean meats, and meat alternatives; create healthy versions of popular Mexican dishes; identify strategies to involve children in healthy cooking; and gain an introductory understanding of basic nutrition.

We lay a foundation during the first class and continue to build on that foundation with each subsequent class, culminating with a graduation lunch that highlights skills learned throughout the entire course. After graduating, the Kitchenistas go out into their community, share their new knowledge, and teach others how to create healthy kitchens within their own homes. After each Cooking for Salud™ session, the new graduates join the Kitchenista alumni for monthly meetings to discuss health and nutrition topics and share healthy recipes, as well as participate in community events.

We believe there are a number of qualities that make the Cooking for Salud™ program successful. Our Theory of Change outlines the specific characteristics that we see as essential for participant investment.

Critical Features of Cooking for Salud™	The theory or principle behind the feature
Led by graduates of previous sessions of the program; Identification	A sense of identification, which is not based solely on being Latina, but also being similar to participants in cultural, economic, and educational backgrounds. (Promotoras Model)
	Adults learn best when they talk to others about their life experiences and engage in dialogue to relate these experiences to the learning process. (Adult Learning Theory)
Small size/ community classes; Most participants are from National City or the South Bay	Community members engage in dialogue to look at root causes of eating habits at home. Participation and relevance/involvement of the community is critical to the change process. Participants are empowered and individuals gain mastery over their lives. (Community Organizing Model)

Critical Features of Cooking for Salud™	The theory or principle behind the feature
Hands-on	People more successfully remember what they learn when they practice or use their learning rather than when they only read or hear information. (Dale's Cone of Learning)
Garden-setting	Environment plays a role in changing behavior. Our unique garden setting for the program makes participants feel special and reminds them of where their food comes from. (Social Cognitive Theory)
Guest Chef volunteers	Participants learn by watching others (experts) and guest chefs are community role models.
Weekly giveaways for participants to practice techniques learned at home	A person's readiness to change their health behaviors are dependent on their perceived barriers (factors such as cost, inconvenience, time) that make it difficult for the individual to change the behavior. Practical examples of how to implement new techniques can improve participants' perceived confidence in the kitchen. (Health Belief Model)
Graduation celebration with presentation where Kitchenistas share their journey and goals for the future	Behavior change is the goal; new practices are often more effective with commitments. Participants deliver a presentation about their experiences and health commitments to other graduates, facilitators, and community members at a luncheon ceremony. Behavior change is a journey, not an event. (Behavior Change Model)
Bilingual instruction	The majority of participants are native Spanish speakers; instruction is provided in English and Spanish to ensure active participation on the part of the learners and to create trust in the learning environment: teacher, class design, objectives.

Our Intended Impacts

Goal #1: Kitchenistas mindfully prepare and consume food. Kitchenistas transform their home kitchen to support healthy eating. Kitchenistas intentionally make healthy eating choices and eat to improve long term health.

Goal #2: Families are engaged in healthy eating decisions and practices. Family members engage in healthy meal planning, ingredient selection, and meal preparation.

Goal #3: Kitchenistas are ambassadors of healthy eating in their family and community. Kitchenistas develop confidence to share new healthy strategies with their family and the community.

Methodology

We spent the past seven months evaluating and refining our intended impacts and indicators. The aim of our evaluation was to see what kind and quality of impact Cooking for Salud™ has on its participants. To assess the success of the program in achieving our intended impacts, we developed an in-depth interview protocol to capture qualitative data and a detailed retrospective survey to capture quantitative data.

Using the Heart Triangle[1] method of evaluation that attempts to uncover transformational changes, we developed a 20 question in-depth interview protocol (10 sequences of questions). Each question sequence asked Kitchenistas to first reflect on any changes in their knowledge, actions, or feelings; and secondly to delve deeper to assess if they experienced any changes in their beliefs, habits, or acceptance and sense of ownership and agency related to health, nutrition, and community leadership. To effectively reach our Kitchenista population, which consists largely of mono-lingual Spanish speakers, we translated our protocol into Spanish.

Based on previous quantitative surveys of the Kitchenistas, we purposefully stratified our sample to ensure representation of the entire Kitchenista population. Our total Kitchenista population size was 103 and our sample size was 14. Using the demographic data submitted by participants before each class, we drew our sample from the following strata: high/low socioeconomic status, small/large family size, native language, and program graduation date.

---

1. **Patty, Steve**. 2013. *Getting to What Matters: How to design and develop evaluation.* Portland, OR: DIA

Each interview was conducted in approximately one hour and was either a one-on-one or small group (no more than three) interview. The interviews were conducted in the Kitchenista's native language by trained native Spanish-speaking, bilingual volunteers. Olivewood staff trained two volunteers, including a graduate student, Clara Estrella-Varela, interning with San Diego County's South Region Health and Human Services Agency and Kitchenista Esperanza Guerrero from the sixth generation, to use the Heart Triangle method to interview and evaluate data. In addition, Clara assisted with the translation of materials and interviews from English to Spanish and vice versa.

Data was captured through vigorous note-taking during the interview, either by the interviewer or a second support interviewer in the small groups. These were augmented immediately following the interview to include details such as body language assessments and initial thoughts regarding the interview. Interviews done in Spanish were translated into English for analysis.

We began to uncover themes that permeated throughout the conversations with the Kitchenistas. To do this, we sorted through the responses provided by each participant and formed descriptions (what changes occurred as a result of the program, how they occurred, and why they occurred) to categorize significant ideas. We then interpreted each of these descriptions and identified various themes regarding participant changes. We evaluated the themes that persisted throughout the interviews and developed our most significant findings.

In addition to the qualitative in-depth interviews, we developed an anonymous short questionnaire to collect quantitative data on our indicators of impact. This instrument consisted of short answer questions, a retrospective likert scale response, and multiple choice questions. The analysis of this data provided quantitative results to corroborate our qualitative findings. We administered the questionnaire to all seven generations of Cooking for Salud™ graduates, a total of 103 Kitchenistas, in both an online and paper-pencil format and we received 25 responses.

Findings

Finding #1: *"If at first you don't succeed, pick yourself up and try again."*
Participants develop resilience in their journey toward health.

Participants in Cooking for Salud™ regularly stated that they were more confident about becoming healthy because they knew that diet is a collection of lifelong choices, rather than a regimented collection of steps in one direction. If they indulged one day, they could continue the next day making healthy choices so that their general trend was toward better eating. Participants gave themselves permission to make mistakes. Resiliency played a significant role in the success of Kitchenistas in incorporating health into their lives. Kitchenistas reported coming up against a number of obstacles, some personal struggles, and others related to acceptance of healthy changes and new foods by family members. Graduates also cited obstacles such as limited access to grocery stores with fresh produce in close proximity to their homes and a higher cost for organic and other more nutritious ingredients. To overcome her family's pushback, Kathy[2] tells her children "it might not look pretty, but you need to try it." Like other Kitchenistas, she recognizes that change needs to happen slowly and she introduces new things one at a time, not expecting her family to accept new foods immediately.

> "Sometimes it costs more, but I use it (organic produce). I look for cheaper organic options." —*Sofia*

> "I changed my grocery store from Vons to Trader Joe's and Sprouts because they have more of an organic selection." —*Valentina*

Our Response

During each class session, we will maintain structured opportunities for Kitchenistas to discuss the obstacles they are coming up against and give support and advice for overcoming them. Using the data gathered from this report, we will structure discussions around the most commonly encountered challenges for this population.

---

2. Participant names have been changed to protect each Kitchenista's identity.

Reported obstacles to healthy eating

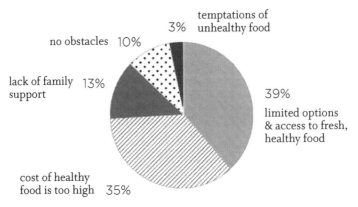

Finding #2: *Si se puede!*
Confidence is an essential trait in making behavior change.

Participants of Cooking for Salud™ stated that their confidence for preparing healthy meals for their family was growing. They are taking risks and trying out new recipes with their family members. Many participants stated that they don't even need a recipe to follow, that they are confident enough to make a meal or invent a new dish without the help of a recipe. Many participants stated that their husbands or children were resistant to changing their eating habits and they struggled to find healthy dishes that their family members would enjoy. After this program, participants reported that they have tried many different strategies to incorporate healthy meals into their family meal preparation routines. Camila stated that she "substituted soy for chorizo" in tacos and her children didn't even notice. Luciana stated that she gets inventive by sneaking in veggies into smoothies for her children or even blending up veggies before adding them to rice. Martina stated that she made a "barbacoa with eggplant instead of meat."

Most of the participants report that they made substitutions to items that their family members previously enjoyed, such as soda, salt, or meat. They build confidence through the satisfaction of knowing that their family members are eating healthier, and they feel good about making healthier choices and substitutions. Julieta expressed, "I know

I am giving my family something healthy and nutritious. I know that it is good even though they would prefer a hamburger."

Family Member Habit Changes	% of Participants that Reported Change
More fruits, veggies, whole grains	72%
More water	36%
Being adventurous, willing to try new foods	20%
Less takeout, more food at home	16%
Less salt, sugar, processed foods	8%
Reading labels	8%
Involving others in healthy eating	4%
Starting a garden	4%

"My husband is sharing recipes with his sister because they are both diabetic. He even makes suggestions about what kitchenware is needed at the store." —*Natalia*

"I want to be more cautious so my children learn for themselves to distinguish what is healthy and what is not." —*Camila*

Some participants have reported that they are sharing recipes and strategies they've learned with others who haven't taken the class. Natalia shared that she spent hours in the grocery store sharing recipes with other patrons. Camila stated that she has been asked to "sell" her food and Daniela stated that her daughter created stickers for her to label her food when giving to others.

Significance

Self-efficacy is one of the most important characteristics that determine behavioral change. The Kitchenistas are finding ways to incorporate healthy habits into their daily lives despite the obstacles they face because they have built a repertoire of skills and strategies through their experience in Cooking for Salud. Kitchenistas are likely to make lasting behavior changes; their confidence is high because they are equipped with the tools they need to make food that their family will enjoy and they are satisfied in knowing that their food will improve the long term health of their family.

Our Response

As an organization, we plan to equip the Kitchenista alumni with training opportunities, curriculum, and presentation strategies to allow them to share their knowledge with the community. We plan to support the Kitchenistas to empower them as community ambassadors who speak with PTO and PTA organizations at local schools, teach healthy cooking classes for faith-based organizations, and lead healthy cooking demonstrations at large community events.

Finding #3: *Different strokes, for different folks.*
Socioeconomic or cultural differences affect participant outcomes.

Often, citizenship, language, and education levels are barriers to long-term health that the Latino population faces. Cooking for Salud™ is facilitated by Latina women who are former graduates of the program. The vast majority of the participants in Cooking for Salud™ are Latina women, thus the participants identify culturally with the leaders of the program. Furthermore, based on their work experience with the community, the participants view these Kitchenista leaders as not only health advocates and educators, but as mentors and inspirations.

> "Hearing the stories form the other ladies was inspiring to hear because I saw that they tried it and it worked, so I tried it. I was hesitant before." —*Lucia*

> "I felt inspired by Paula's story about how she lost weight."
> —*Martina*

Alternatively, after having discussions with participants from a variety of socioeconomic/educational backgrounds, it became clear that these differences affected the participant's outcomes.

In conversations with Kitchenistas from higher socioeconomic backgrounds (typically bilingual or monolingual English speakers), participants reported that they were already committed to a healthier diet for themselves and/or for their families. They reported that the class provided them with new strategies and skills for cooking at home, and they made improvements to their routines. Luciana reported that her husband is very "healthy" and is "supportive" of healthy meals and a healthy lifestyle. She said he eats "everything" she cooks. Renata described her experience in Cooking for Salud™ as "pretty set in the realm of food" and that she didn't take away too many other lessons about health. She stated that she was already very set in her role as the decision maker in her family about food and meals.

In conversations with participants from lower socioeconomic backgrounds (typically monolingual, native Spanish speakers), it was reported that they had a much more difficult time receiving support from their family members, while these participants seem to seek approval from their picky family members as a way of determining whether or not they are successful in creating an enjoyable meal. Natalia laughed, "I had the most trouble with the husband." Many Kitchenistas described similar challenges and often state that their husbands are reluctant to try new recipes. "Even if they go for pizza, I'm still making a salad or a smoothie," stated Julieta about her experiences with her family members. There were many participants who expressed satisfaction and confidence about their journey towards health when their family members reported that they enjoyed the meal. Camila said that she feels "glad" when her family says thank you and that they liked the meal. Many participants report that although it wasn't easy, they are making little changes here and there to eliminate sugar sweetened beverages and frying and have increased fruit and vegetable consumption.

Significance

Participants from different backgrounds face unique challenges around health. Some participants face a steep uphill battle to change their daily habits and their family routine as a result of lack of access to nutrition education and years of cultural influences around food and family structure. Although some participants from higher socioeconomic homes did not report a transformative change in family health habits, the participants from monolingual, lower socioeconomic homes likely would not have made these changes to their family's diets if it was not for the skills and strategies they learned in Cooking for Salud™. In the long term, this suggests decreased likelihood of participants and families from lower socioeconomic backgrounds suffering from diet-related diseases and conditions.

Our Response

While we recognize that women from all socioeconomic backgrounds and neighborhoods benefit from lessons learned through Cooking for Salud™, we see the greatest impacts occur for women coming from lower socioeconomic families. Due to this, we intend to structure future classes to prioritize low-income families that are National City residents or residents from other South Bay communities.

Finding #4: *It worked.*
Participants DID change their eating habits.

Throughout the Cooking for Salud™ course, participants learn new cooking techniques to incorporate more fruits, vegetables, and healthy grains into meals, to reduce the use of salt, sugar, and unhealthy oils, and to make informed, conscious choices about what they consume. They learn that eating healthy can also taste good. Through speaking with graduates of the program, we are seeing that they are, in fact, changing their eating habits.

Kitchenistas noted a number of changes they have made, as well as new techniques and ingredients they are trying out, including reducing or eliminating soda, using more vegetables instead of more meat, and substituting healthier alternatives such as brown rice for white rice. In addition, Kitchenistas report they are using their newfound knowledge to make healthy changes to traditional Mexican dishes. Rather than giving up on important cultural traditions and dishes that have been passed down over the generations, they are making small changes and substitutions, recognizing that this may alter the flavor but it will ultimately make it healthier.

"I cook more frequently; 4 or 5 days a week rather than going out almost every day." —*Emma*

"I do not keep soda in the house anymore." —*Camila*

These are not just changes in the way Kitchenistas cook, they are changes in the way they view and approach food and meal preparation. They feel confident to make new meals and they consider health and nutrition when making purchases in the grocery store. They recognize why eating for health is important and are more comfortable and more inclined to make decisions about what they eat based on what is healthier. Isabel stated that her "stomach seems to reject bad food" now that she has changed her diet to incorporate healthier options. Kathy talked about how she used to "just look at the price" when making purchase decisions, but now she "buys what is healthier, regardless of the price."

I eat fruits and vegetables as part of every meal

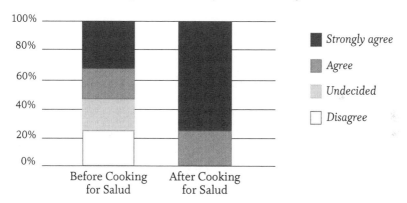

Significance

Kitchenistas are incorporating what they have learned into daily life. Their new knowledge and skills have transformed into habits that affect their personal and family health. One of the goals of the Cooking for Salud™ program is that Kitchenistas will mindfully prepare and consume food. This finding demonstrates that program graduates are making an effort to consider their food choices, both at the grocery store when making purchases and at home when making meals. This is significant as it indicates that tangible change has occurred in the eating habits of Kitchenistas. In the long term, this suggests decreased likelihood of participants suffering from diet-related diseases and conditions.

Our Response

We plan to maintain and continue to offer the strategies and tools that are built into the current instruction, as this data confirms that our curriculum is effective. Thanks to the support from culinary experts, chef volunteers and local restaurants, we plan to provide regular electives for Kitchenistas after graduating. Canning and preserving classes, tours of local markets and produce warehouses, visits to local gardens and restaurants, and in-depth nutrition informational sessions will be held as continuing educational opportunities.

Finding #5: *"Now that you know, you can't go back."*
Health is now a goal and a driving value in their life.

For the majority of the women entering the Cooking for Salud™ program, basic knowledge about health and nutrition is limited. Many of the women state that they had given into the idea that they would get diabetes or cancer because their parents or aunts and uncles had. This was viewed as fate, rather than a consequence of eating behaviors. In fact, food is often viewed as a means to an end where families pick up fast food meals because they do not have time or have not prioritized making meals at home. Other times, families are making meals passed on through generations and do not consider the health ramifications. Participants of Cooking for Salud™ have expressed feeling guilty about changing the recipes of their mothers and grandmothers. Despite this, we were told in interview after interview that "once you know, you can't go back."

> "We have taken it up a notch at home. We walk to school and limit what snacks are bought at the grocery store." —*Luciana*

> "Now I see ladies in the stores with boxes of juices and I say to myself: that used to be me." —*Julieta*

As a result of what they've learned in Cooking for Salud™, Kitchenistas feel that it is their responsibility to make health a priority in their lives. After learning about the negative health impacts of sugar, the importance of eating a balanced diet, and how to read a nutrition label, participants recognize they cannot unlearn this - they are now compelled to make decisions that support health. Health has become a value, in addition to a practice. One participant went so far as to say, "People don't die, they kill themselves" referring to food related illnesses and diseases. Now that participants are aware of the consequences of eating poorly, as well as the benefits of eating well, it is difficult for them to imagine going back. They can no longer avoid or ignore health or the influence food plays on health.

My family prioritizes health

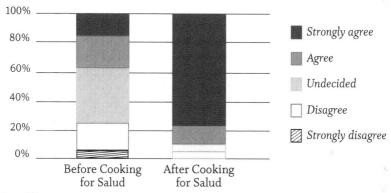

Significance

Participants feel very strongly about the value of health. They truly believe in the importance of making health a priority and recognize that they have a responsibility in ensuring that the food they eat not only tastes good, but is good for them. For most of the participants, this feeling extended beyond themselves and onto their families. They want health to be a priority for other family members and they hope their commitment to making healthy decisions will transfer to others.

Our Response

Using the "Parking Lot" model, we will provide an opportunity for participants to ask questions regarding nutrition, ingredients, etc.

throughout the course of the program. Participants will have an opportunity to post questions they have throughout the course and on the last class, a guest nutrition expert will speak to the class and address the questions they pose.

Finding #6: *Mi Salud es su Salud.*
Personal, family, and community health are all connected.

Cooking for Salud™ participants join for a variety of reasons. For some, it is a desire to learn new cooking techniques, for others it is to lose weight, for others it is to improve the health of a pre-diabetic child. Regardless of the reason, most participants discovered through the course that we are all connected in our health journey. To desire and strive for personal health, it is almost impossible not to affect those around us - our family and our community. When health becomes a priority, it becomes almost impossible to not want to affect and improve the health of our family and community. Conversely, participants that joined the course to improve their family's health found they themselves also could improve and were inspired to do so.

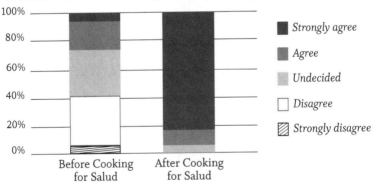

I feel confident in sharing healthy eating with the community

There are a number of factors that connect us: the food system, cultural traditions, family dynamics—and all these are tied together by the food we eat. Many participants not only are working to improve the health of their families, but are actively sharing recipes and healthy cooking techniques learned through the course with their friends and communities.

Significance

At Olivewood, we aim to affect change one family at a time. Cooking for Salud™ is doing just that, and the ripple effects of working with the stewards of family health - in this case the mothers and grandmothers in our community - are widespread. Kitchenistas are not only changing their personal health outcomes, but those of their family and community.

Our Response

Participants in Cooking for Salud™ will be provided with opportunities to engage with the community during the seven-week course. For example, participants will be invited to attend a volunteer orientation to support them in helping hands-on cooking classes for school students at Olivewood Gardens. In addition, participants will also be engaged in supporting school and community garden projects.

Finding # 7: *Eat, live, love.*
Food is an integral component to a sense of life satisfaction and purpose.

Cooking for Salud™ celebrates cultural traditions but acknowledges the need to revise diets to accommodate new realities of daily life such as greater access to high calorie foods and reduced physical activity. We propose that food preparation is an aspect of cultural transmission that, without it, many people feel disconnected from their communities and from their families. When this practice is restored in some part, participants feel more satisfied with themselves and more connected to their families.

> Luciana says, "Losing food is like losing culture; I've learned ways to keep traditions and be healthy. Cooking is culture, is family, is tradition, is love."

When looking for connections and themes throughout the qualitative interview data, many participants commented on a sense of resilience, confidence, and greater connection to their family or community that comes from feeling empowered to make healthy dietary decisions and mindfully creating healthy meals. Participants are making a link between mindful food preparation and life satisfaction and purpose. Food preparation and enjoyment become ways to demonstrate love for family and to develop resilience and confidence that trickles into other family dynamics and other aspects of participants' lives.

Furthermore, familial and community pride is often drawn from the ability of members to create delicious, healthy versions of traditional favorites. Several Kitchenistas mentioned the pride they felt when they provided for their family in a healthy way, giving nourishment and a gift of time and health. Kitchenistas report family and friends complimenting them on the food they bring to parties, because it was delicious and homemade, in addition to being healthy.

Significance

This finding illustrates that an emotional connection to healthy eating is established and reinforced through the preparation and appreciation of family meals and celebration foods. Promoting this mindful preparation and consumption of food seems to cement the transition between eating healthy once in a while to living a healthy lifestyle every day. It associates love for your family with the desire to an act of feeding them healthy food, and positively reinforces self confidence in the preparers when people notice their efforts.

Our Response

This messaging of "food as love" seems already apparent at some level in the delivery of the program but it may be worth facilitating discussions with key phrases such as "Show Your Love", for example, to tap into the natural desire to please and provide for one's family and community. We can also make participants feel special by providing similar praise to the students through encouraging notes or small gifts each week. We will also ensure that the program incorporates strategies to encourage keeping cultural traditions alive and celebrating with family in healthy ways.

Finding #8: *"Honey, we forgot the kids!"*
With our current program model, family involvement is difficult to achieve.

One of our program goals is that Families are engaged in healthy eating decisions and practices. We discovered that although most participants expressed success in their goal of building healthier habits for their family, this was often a result of the Kitchenistas taking control of the decision making around food. We realized that in our current curriculum structure we did not build in enough opportunity to practice or motivate participants to invite their families into the cooking process. Although one participant reported that "my husband cuts up the tomatoes, the cucumber, and my son helps with the lemons," there was not a trend to indicate that this was happening in all of the participants' homes. In addition, the program does not offer direct instruction on how to incorporate children and family into the cooking process.

Significance

To build family cohesion and for healthy habits to be ingrained into the family lifestyle, the Cooking for Salud™ program should provide explicit instruction, models and examples of ways for parents to incorporate children into the cooking process. When children and family members are involved in the cooking process, they are more likely to take risks and try new foods, and are likely to take accountability for their healthy eating choices. Moving forward, we will discuss ways to improve our program model to help participants engage family members in healthy meal planning, ingredient selection, and meal preparation.

Our Response

Up to this point, discussions about inviting family members into the kitchen have been nominal and have taken place informally while chefs have been working with the Kitchenistas with other primary goals in mind. We propose building in this conversation and practice more overtly, perhaps through a Family Field Trip or other whole family visit opportunity designed to introduce everyone to the healthy meal preparation process. We also need to examine the process of introducing new healthy foods to family members, sharing helpful strategies, the types of responses change-makers can expect to contend with, and appropriate responses to resistant family members.

Steps Forward

For our upcoming Fall 2016 session of Cooking for Salud™, we plan to strengthen our program by making the following adjustments.

1. **Add an opportunity to bring participants' families to visit the garden, introduce basic food awareness, the principles of the class, and simple cooking skills that everyone can do.** By sharing with their children or spouses what the class participants have been up to, we may be able to compel family members to support them through their journey and/ or become more engaged themselves in the change process. We aim to structure this experience so that participants guide their family members, putting them in the role of mentor for their families.

2. **Prioritize admission for participants who are low-income and from National City or the South Bay.** Cooking for Salud™ was originally envisioned as a forum for uniting parents around a common goal - to improve the health of their families by empowering them to more mindfully prepare food at home. However, this cohesion did not really occur, and participants from outside of National City from higher socioeconomic backgrounds were less likely to stay engaged with the group afterward. In this next series, we will prioritize admission to National City and South Bay residents. In the future, we plan to develop an application process that provides the option for potential participants to disclose income levels.

3. **Formalize discussions about obstacles to behavior change and how to overcome them.** Participants point to difficulties convincing their spouses and older children to change their

eating behaviors, as well as issues related to access and accessibility of healthy foods. In addition to informal idea sharing that always takes part in the class, we will build in facilitated discussion time to acknowledge this challenge and brainstorm ways to get around them.

EDUCATION | CHARACTER DEVELOPMENT | LEADERSHIP

Pro Kids | The First Tee of San Diego

Pro Kids Academy

Kathy Wilder

Chief Operating Officer

Katie Lynch

Director – Oceanside

Our Purpose

Pro Kids was founded in 1994 by Ernie Wright, a former Chargers football player, and his dedicated staff. Ernie opened the doors of Pro Kids at the Colina Park Golf Course in City Heights in partnership with the City of San Diego and Callaway Golf. At the time, the City Heights was a community of crime with 37 established gangs and the highest youth-related arrest and homicide rates in the county. Pregnancy rates for girls ages 15-19 also topped county charts at 21 percent. City Heights was a community divided, as both families and youth struggled to find place, identity and a network of support. Pro Kids served as a safe haven, providing shelter, engaging activity and mentorship. In 2012, Ernie's vision was fulfilled when we expanded to our second site in Oceanside. We took a close look at our purpose in our communities and the impact we were having on our members and families. The following was at the center of our organization's work and purpose:

Why we are here

We believe that all children and youth deserve equal access to resoures and experiences necessary to excel in life.

WHAT we do

We challenge underserved youth to excel in life by promoting character development, life-skills, and values through education and the game of golf.

WHO we are

We are a lead organization in San Diego County providing opportunity, hope and voice to underserved and marginalized communities.

Our Strategy

What is the Smash Factor?

"Smash factor measures how much power is transferred from the club to the ball. The biggest key to a high smash factor is striking the ball on its center at the right angle with the most control. This maximizes the energy transfer sending the ball to its greatest distance on the truest course." — *Trackman News, May 2008*

Our primary strategic program, the Pro Kids Academy, is intended to maximize the smash factor of our work with the most vulnerable members. The Academy intends to provide a structured, attendance based after school program that will close the resource gap, preparing these members to go the greatest distance on their truest course.

Restructuring Pro Kids to the Academy model meant building on our current curriculum and program with an increasing focus on accountability to measurably grow our impact and deliver better outcomes. Implementation of Pro Kids Academy (PKA) shifted our orientation from transactional to intentional; to best meet community needs, graduation from high school – and college and career readiness.

Prime Directive and Member Initiative

We started the process by establishing a practical prime directive and member centered initiative for our work. This directly connects to the heart of our strategic planning process:

Prime Directive: Pro Kids members will graduate high school with the habits, skills and relationships to succeed with a post-secondary plan.

Member Initiative: Build habits, skills and supporting relationships to be effective and confident students and community members.

Intended Impacts

We anticipated the following impact as a result of our organizational transformation and implementation of Pro Kids Academy:

1. **Members build trusting, supportive relationships with adults.**

2. **Members take responsibility for their own lives.** Members demonstrate accountability with commitments, ability to work independently and collaboratively with a group.

3. **Members have a strong sense of community and pride.** Members know that Pro Kids is "a place where I belong".

4. **Members are college and career ready.** Members show improved performance and confidence in a school/professional setting, including completing assigned work, communication with teachers and adults as well as commitment to working hard

Overview

This research process aimed to provide findings to drive future actions in response to the experience and feedback of our members and parents. We looked at the intended impact of the Academy program as compared to the experiences and perspectives of members and parents after the first year of implementation. We were able to examine the impact of the Academy in both the short term, for the first year, and comparatively for those who had been Pro Kids members in prior years. Some sixth grade members had participated in ProKids for up to five years prior to the inception of the Academy.

Research Highlights

Findings revealed both positive feedback and constructive suggestions to further develop the program. This is a snapshot of the findings that will be discussed at greater length later in this report.

> ➤ Members consistently reported being more prepared and commited as students.

> ➤ Members reported that the structure of the Academy was challenging and sometimes hard; however, they appreciated and could explain the connection between the structure of the teams and the positive experience of having increased success in school.

> ➤ Members reported having better relationships and experiences with siblings at home. They were able to articulate the experience of being a part of an Academy team and how this helped them be a better brother or sister.

> ➤ Parents reported members being more helpful and involved at home since they started Pro Kids, and even more so since joining the Academy. For example, parents noticed their child going out of their way to help a sibling, or assist with meal prep or clean up.

> ➤ Parents reported having to use less guidance and direction at home, noticing that their child was more proactive. For example, a parent reported that their child loved to read before bed, so bed time was easier. She would have to go to his room to find him tucked in and reading almost everynight.

> ➤ Members reported a feeling of disconnection from the greater Pro Kids community since the start of the Academy teams, with an expressed desire to have more generalized interaction with other age groups.

> ➢ Parents reported a need for more homework time and more speciality tutoring for members who were either below grade level proficiency or greatly exceeding profiency.

These findings will build both the foundation of the Academy program and the scaffolding of the expansion of the program in years to come. We intend to share these results with potential donors, existing partners as well as parents, staff and volunteers. As refleced in the action section of this report, modifications are already underway in the program based on the valuable information gathered during this process.

Methodology

Development of the tools used to conduct the evaluation of programmatic impact required the creation of the appropriate question and discussion of the process of both in person interviews as well as independent surveys. First, qualitative interviews were conducted with small groups. The quantitative survey was distributed to members and parents through the online program, Survey Monkey. There was minor overlap in questions between the two tools.

Qualitative Inteviews

Our sample included 12 Academy members, six from each site. All members were enrolled in the Pro Kids Academy during the 2015-16 school year. Qualitative interviews were conducted in a group format with the goal of helping the kids feel more comfortable and open to sharing. 35 questions were included on the protocols list.

Members struggled with the length of the interview process and needed stretch breaks thorughout the process Overall the participants expressed positive feelings about being a part of the interview and spending time with a staff member. Members took the process seriously. This vehicle of the questions and the interview format was a positive way to connect with members. This experience also appeared to empower the members to honestly share opinions and solutions for the program beyond the interview session.

Quantitative Survey

The Survey Monkey format was distributed by hand to parents and faciliated by team leaders in the Academy groups. This distribution occurred after the completion of the qualitative interviews. 32 respondents participated, 28 parents and four members. Some surveys were conducted by hard copy to meet the needs of the parents. The purpose of this survey was to retrieve metric based data to compare, contrast and support the qualitative findings of the interviews.

Lessons and Limitations

➤ Creating more "kid friendly" tools would provide more authentic data, with less explanation from the person facilitating the survey. Parent distribution could start earlier and be a requirement of all Academy parent.

➤ Members who were able to sit for the interviews are a sample of the more controlled, well-behaved members. This could impact results as it is not a true sample of members participating in the Academy.

➤ When put in a situation where feedback is asked for, most of the members were very honest about experience, feedback and even solutions.

➤ A warm up activity that will help the members loosen up both emotionally and physcially prior to the interview would assist in the authenticity and richness of the survey.

➤ Parent experience some limitation when accessing computers from home. Computer stations available for use and a concerted promotion of the quantitative survey at the parent nights leading up to end of the school year would help with getting a larger sample.

➤ Access to materials in other languages would have opened the process to more of our famlies. Offering multiple languages including Spanish, Somali and Vietmanese in the future will broaden our pool.

➤ Sample size in general is very small. While that was expected this year during the development phase, results would be more meaningful if the sample size included at least 50% of the participating members and parents.

Our Findings

In connection to the prime directive, the member intiative and our intended impacts, the following relevant themes emerged from the research.

Finding #1: *Growth Mindset - Members developed a greater commitment and preparedness for school and future planning*

Academy members consistently reported being more prepared and commited as students as well as experiencing greater success at school through grades citizenship and verbal praise from teachers. Several members were able to describe the moment of change from not caring to caring about doing homework and doing well. A sixth grader reported that before joining his team, he never thought about the future or even his homework. He remembered his Team Leader saying that doing homework well is like doing well practice for doing your job well in the future. He reported having a sense of pride in completing his homework everyday and doing better in school. He also stated that he planned to go to college.

90% of parent respondents agree or strongly agree that their child knows what they want to do after high school. A parent of a sixth grader stated "We never thought that our kids would want to go to college. Now they talk about it all the time."

Significance

Academy members in the 6th grade averaged 64% proficiency in Math and 63% in literacy, exceeding their peers from local middle schools who ranked 34% proficiency in Math and 42% in literacy. (Great School, n.d.) The growth mindset theory, as presented by Dweck (2006), is the belief that change in ability, circumstances, performance and opportunity is possible. According to Dweck (2006) developing growth mindset in the context of underserved and marginalized populations is especially important to sustain long term success. This finding is demonstrating a change in regular practice and belief, starting with the member's ability to complete homework and finish tasks indepedently as well as look forward to a future that includes post secondary planning.

2016 Grade Level Proficiency Comparison

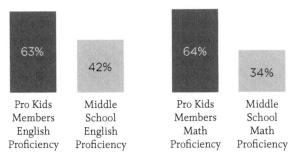

| Pro Kids Members English Proficiency | Middle School English Proficiency | Pro Kids Members Math Proficiency | Middle School Math Proficiency |

Finding #2: *Getting Gritty - Members embraced challenges, even when it was hard.*

Members were able to articulate that the structure of the Academy was challenging and sometimes hard to the point of dislike. They could also express appreciation for and could explain the connection between the structure of the teams and the positive experience of having increased success with personal organization, school and home life. A sixth grader reported that at first he didn't like doing daily enrichment tasks, in addition to his school work. After time, he could see his math grade improve and wasn't always rushed to finish his work in class. He expressed gratitude for being pushed to do more. He reported feeling more excited about math, even though he didn't feel he was strong in the subject. He knew he could do well if he worked hard enough.

A fifth grader reported that she always felt overwhelmed afterschool, and didn't know how to get her work done. With the help of her team leader she figured out that working on the hardest problems first was the best, and asking for help with pronouncing and learning new words. She reported that since English isn't her Mom's first language she never got anything right on her English homework until she started doing it daily at Pro Kids. Now she is teaching her mom some English.

88% of parent respondents strongly agree that their child is a better student. A parent attributed her child's improvement her ability to keep going on projects or assignments even when they are difficult. Her child was doing much better with completing homework and reading assignments completely. Another parent described a team leader's help teaching her child about project management. She stated "My daughter didn't know how to do an eight-week science project, she was totally overwhelmed. With the help of her team leader she was able to learn about being organized and doing one thing at a time to get it done. She got an A on the project, it was a big boost for her."

Significance

Often parents do not have the language skills, time due to work or the experience with the education system in general to effectively help with homework and build good study habits. As stated in the prime directive and member intiative, building positive habits is even more of an important cornerstone than having excellent grades. Duckworth (2016) found in her research around the Grit Theory that deliberate practice and positive habits have longer lasting and more integrated results than academic performance. Encouraging an ethic of hardwork and personal effort is directly tied to preparing our members to succeed in life.

Relationships Matter! Pro-social development transferred to home and school.

The majority of the member interviewees spoke about having better relationships and experiences with siblings at home. They were able to express the experience of being a part of a team and how this helped them tolerate and even like their siblings. Members reported having increased patience, more appreciation , more ability to "go with the flow" and more desire to help, especially in regards to younger siblings. A sixth grade member talked about being less anxious about spending time away from his older brother, knowing that he had made a friend (his first friend) at Pro Kids.

73% of the parent respondents reported that they agree or strongly agree that their children have become more confident people. This confidence manifests itself in better relationships and improved social interaction. This includes seven response from parents who had members Pro Kids prior to the Academy. A fifth grade parent described using less guidance and direction at home, noticing that their child was more helpful.

Significance

While members will often develop habits and skills in the context of a program or atmosphere, deep-seated learning is demonstrated when similar habits and skills are demonstrated in a new environment. When members start translating learned behaviors and other positive team culture with their families, this is a clear indicator that they are deeply learning the life skills of Pro Kids. Dweck (2006) describes this type of learning as deep saturation, discussing the concept of "second nature".

Finding #3: *Finding and forging identity - Members want to belong*

Description: Members unanimously agreed that they felt loss of generalized identity when moved to team, spending less time with the group as a whole. One sixth grade member described the change as a loss of freedom and friends from other age groups with the Pro Kids community. When pressed further to understand the gaps, members expressed that while they liked spending time with their team leader and their close friends, they did not identify strongly with the team. They expressed a desire to do activities that would bring the team closer, from team competitions to cooperative challenges. Multiple members gave the example of an initiative activity called the "talking ruler". A sixth grade member talked about the talking ruler as a favorite activity. The team sits in a circle and the person with the ruler shares about their day. The member described why he liked this activity saying "we get to talk about ourselves and learn more about other people. Maybe you think that person is not cool, but then you hear about their day and you realize, they are just like me!"

Members crave the opportunity to connect on a deeper level with others. Primarily, they have a desire to connect with peers. However, many members appreciate direct interaction and involvement of the staff and volunteers. A sixth grader offered the suggestion to have more incentives as a team and as an individual using the points system. She reported not feeling motivated to move up in the levels system. The level system is like the martial arts belts system in that members move up in levels by proving improvement in golf and life skills as well as participation in the program.

98% of parent respondents strongly agree that the adults at Pro Kids are committed to the success of their child. A parent of a sixth grader stated that she wants her child to have fun after school and also be safe. At Pro Kids, she felt she was getting the best of both worlds because the adults care and listen. Other parents commented that they would like more time for their children to focus on homework as well as time to socialize with friends. Several parents expressed that they felt suggestions and ideas would be considered if offered by kids or parents to positively change the program.

Significance

The concern with these issues revolved around two central internal metrics. The first is retention and the second is golf skills level progression. The retention of members from prior years to this year is 59% on a goal of 70% by the end of 2016. 100% of the Academy members were Pro Kids members in previous years. Team identity will help retain members, while lack of identity threatens to drive members away. Retaining members for the long term is key to our prime directive which aims to carry members through to high school graduation. Understanding and addressing the need for greater identity forging for teams specifically to maintain current member participation and retain this activity for the next six year must be a programmatic priority.

Currently, the golf level progression rate is at 22% on a goal of 50% by the end of 2016. Academy members are progressing slightly faster at 25%.

The reduction in progression may be an indicator that kids are feeling disjointed from teams or limited by team structure and therefore do not progress. With a greater sense of belonging and team, it seems that members will be more motivated to continue to progress and stick with the program. This is a weaker correlation with identity, but could help to focus staff when addressing the issues at hand when dealing with team development.

Finding #4: *Welcome environment – Parents want to engage and understand the full capacity of the program.*

Many of the members talked about their favorite time at Pro Kids being the times they could bring their parent or guardian to Pro Kids to share their experience. A sixth grader stated "My mom is here all the time, but she had never spent time in the class with me. I loved having her with me so I could show off my art projects and introduce her to my team leader and my group." Parents were overwhelmingly in favor of the positive impact of parent nights and relationships they had developed with staff and volunteers over the last year. One parent stated "Ms. S. has gone out of her way to help my son. She deeply cares about his well-being and how he's doing as a person. He is better off knowing her and so I am I. I know she's there for us."

100% of the parent respondants strongly agree high satisfaction with the program and report re-enrolling next year for the Academy.

Significance

Parental and family engagement can make or break the success of a child. An absentee parent is sometimes preferrable over a parent who is inconsistent as this is a difficult situation to navigate for children and youth. Payne (2000) discusses the importance of consistent parent support and engagement in school. According to her research this is more important than having parents who have obtained post secondary education. Encouragement, attendnace and presence are the three areas she identifies as the keys to successful school support from parents that helps to develop patterns and habits of a good student(Payne, 2000). It is most effective for Pro Kids to work hand in hand with parents and families to address the member initiative of building habits for success.

Conclusions

1. Members are in a more disciplined environment and therefore are experienceing an increase in success and interest in student study skills and academic achievement. Members are expressing greater confidence as students and express personal satisfaction with this success. They are motivated to continue these practices and skills even though they report the practice as challenging and difficult.

2. Team building and establishing team identity is currently lacking. Kids can identify the team, but at this time feel a low level of kinship or connection with others. This dynamic condition is causing a desire move to larger group activities and more freedom to be independent. Increased fun is requested, especially in regards to formal academic programs such as SMASH Labs.

3. Members have an interest in being a part of the solution and building teams. Ideas for improvement in regards to building teams and working toward individual incentives and group accomplishments were brought to the table by the kids. Members also appreciated the role of the team leader as a designated person and look toward that person to guide their Pro Kids experience.

4. Members are able to transfer skills learned at Pro Kids to both school and home. With this transfer of skills, members are able to negotiate the school day and home life better. Members are also able to recognize that they can positively change.

5. Parents can recognize and describe positive changes in their children over the past year. Parents who have been involved in the Academy, have a positive opinion of the program and plan to enroll their children next year. Team leader relationships with parents provide the most direct support for families in context of working with their child.

Steps Forward

Increase academic enrichment and addressing personal organization

Last year only the six grade used directed, measurable enrichment for math and literacy proficiency. This year we will implement enrichment programs at the appropriate volume in all age groups. The success of this program has shown an increase in academic performance as well as self reported improved confidence among Academy members who participated.

Student study skills will be addressed more intentionally, with each member receiving an organizational binder to keep papers and lessons from the program. These binders will serve as portfolios throughout the year to capture the volume and quality of work and how this changes.

Golf Coach and Team Leader Partnership

Golf coaches will be assigned to a specific Academy team to work hand in hand with the team leader. The coach will help develop practice routines and progression plans to help members keep moving forward, challenging them to improve skills and vigilance of practice. While this is not the coaches only responsibility, working with the staff will be a priority

Implementation of Academy Assessment System

Academy member progress will be assessed using a new tool. The tool includes a balance of academic performance, golf progression, leadership and life skills experience, resiliency change and STEM interest. It also includes a final project called the Presentation of Learning in which each student will do a short power point presentation of their year in review. The score from all of these areas will be averaged on a weighed scale and used to assess the effectiveness of the Academy. Members will only see and be incetivised with performance in the individual categories. The academy program expectations and schedule for 2016-17 has been designed around the assessment, beginning with the end in mind (Covey, 2007).

Annual Reporting Practice

Qualitative and quantitative evaluation and research will be implemented as a part of the annual reporting cycle to donors, board members, staff , volunteers and community members. Qualitative interviews will take place biannually.The sample size will be increased next year to 30% of Academy participants

Team building practice and purpose

Teams and sites will implement teambuilding plans along with internal assessment of progress. Plan can include both cooperative challenges and cross group competition. This will be a part of the monthly calendar planning and a priority agenda item a the weekly meetings. The assigned coach will be involved or in support of the team building efforts, with a focus on incorporation of golf. Gruno, J. & Gibbons, S. (2014) discuss the positive outcome of trust and healthy risk taking when teambuilding is properly facilitatied. The authors state " The ability to take risk and trust those around you while doing it is important to development of the body and brain".

References

Duckworth, A. (2016) *Grit.* New York, New York.

Dweck, C. (2006) *Mindset: The New Psychology of Success.* New York, New York.

Paybe, R. (2013) *Framework for Understanding Poverty.* Highlands, Texas.

Great Schools (n.d.) Retrieved from http://www.greatschools.org/. July 20, 2016.

Gruno, J., & Gibbons, S. L. (2014). *Teaching Teambuilding in Physical Education: Supporting*

Trust and Risk. *Physical & Health Education Journal,* 80(1), 6-17.

Hospice of the North Coast

Bereavement Counseling

Jim Reiser
Social Services Manager

Sharon Lutz
Executive Director

Cathy Gibson
Patient Care Manager

Cyndie Acosta
Volunteer Coordinator

Acknowledgement

We at Hospice of the North Coast would like to thank and acknowledge our community, and the many families that have allowed us to share the precious moments at the end of life, and to continue to support them through their grief. We also want to thank the 23 survivors with whom we provided individual counseling, and who were gracious enough to share their time and bare their souls.

A great deal of thanks goes to Steve Patty and Jessamyn Luiz from DIA, whose patience and wonderful teaching methods opened our minds to greater possibilities and techniques to help patients and survivors through the difficult challenges that we all face at the end of life. We are grateful for your vision, heart, and talent that has directed you to effect positive change in the world.

Lastly, this would not have happened if not for the Gumpert Foundation's forward thinking and generous financial support. Thank you David Cornsweet and Patrick Dempsey! I also have to include our executive director at Hospice of the North Coast, Sharon Lutz. It takes a leader with a clear heart, purpose and vision to seize opportunities like this and allow it to happen!

Executive Summary

Hospice of the North Coast (HNC) is a Not-For-Profit hospice that has served the north San Diego County region since 1981. In addition to medical, social services, and spiritual care, all hospices are mandated to provide bereavement services, set forth by the Conditions of Participation (COP's) determined by the Center for Medicare & Medicaid Services (CMS). CMS is the largest source of funding for the hospice industry. In 2010 it was estimated that the Medicare payments for hospice services was approximately $13 billion (NHPCO, NHPCO's acts and firgures: Hopsice cae in America, 2014).

The COP for bereavement does not specify the type of services a hospice should provide, and it varies from hospice to hospice. It can be as minimal as one phone call, and servicing only the patient's family, to a much wider scope of services and larger service base than just hospice patients and their families. At Hospice of the North Coast, we have always maintained a robust bereavement program offered to our patients, their families and friends, and to our community. We provide follow up phone calls, a monthly newsletter, individual counseling, group counseling, and pre-bereavement for patients and families. We also provide three bereavement events per year open to the community that celebrates the lives of their loved ones, and give them access to a positive grieving process.

The purpose of this report was to clarify the impact we desired for our bereaved clients in individual counseling, and to measure that impact through personal qualitative interviews. We believed that we helped the bereaved through support, and that counseling with a Marriage Family Therapist Trainee or Intern was a focused process that normalized, and guided the individual and/or family through this struggle. We had used quantitative questionnaires in the past which mostly measured their appreciation for the service. This process forced us to think deeper about the impact we wanted our counseling program to make. We began by discussing what we wanted to achieve with our clients through the grieving process. We asked "what did we want them to leave with?" and "what could be the possible reason for the grieving process?" It was through this discussion and analysis that we came up with our intended impact for people suffering grief.

Our Intended Impact: The bereaved are enriched through the grieving experience.

We defined this as those that are grieving the loss of a loved one, transform their lives by deconstructing the life they knew and rebuilding it through choice into a life they desire and love. To see them active in their lives, and assimilating changes that enhance their self-concept. In short, they would become someone different than they were, and the change would be positive for them.

We conducted 23 face to face interviews of HNC family members and friends, as wells as, Community clients that used our counseling services within the past calendar year (between January 2015 through December 2015). A nine question survey was created to gather quantitative and qualitative data. We found that people were enriched through the grieving process, as 13 of the 23 exhibited qualities of enrichment. Enrichment was judged by how the process changed their life in a positive way so that they were living a life that brings them joy. They used statements such as "I have become grateful for the pain of her death, which brought me to a new realization" or, "I was afraid of what grief could be, but now I love the opportunities I have now."

We also found areas within the process to study so that we can make a more concerted effort on behalf of those that seek help. This study has opened more avenues to how we may approach our work and facilitate positive change and achieve our impact goal.

Introduction

In 1967, Dame Cicely Saunders, a physician, created St. Christopher's Hospice in a suburb of London England. Dame Saunders had been interested in providing specialized care for the dying beginning in 1948. Florence Wald, who was dean of nursing at Yale University took an interest and went to London to study "hospice" care at St. Christopher's. About this same time Elizabeth Kubler-Ross did a comprehensive study of 500 dying patients and established the "five stages of grief" in her published best seller "On Death and Dying", which is still in print today. In 1972, Dr. Kubler-Ross was invited to testify before the U.S. senate on how we isolate the dying and by so doing strip them of their dignity and hinder a peaceful dying process in which the patient's wishes are expressed and followed, which would allow them a peaceful and fulfilling dying process.

The hospice movement started gaining traction as Florence Wald retuned from London to start the first hospice in the U.S. with two physicians, and a chaplain. This hospice is Connecticut Hospice which was founded in 1974. It was in 1982 that Medicare began a hospice benefit, and in 1986 they made it a permanent fixture as a Medicare benefit (NHPCO, History of Hospice Care, 2016).

Hospice of the North Coast is one of 5800 hospices in the U.S. that cares for approximately 1.5 million patients, according to the National Hospice and Palliative Care Organization (NHPCO) estimates from 2013.

Our mission is to provide compassionate personalized care to patients and families during the end-of-life transition.

HNC was established in 1980 and reorganized as an independent agency, licensed by the State of California and certified by Medicare in 1989. Since then, HNC has provided hospice services, counseling services, support and education to thousands of children, teens, adults and elderly within the north San Diego County community.

Methodology

A qualitative interview protocol with nine sequences of questions was used to elicit qualitative data (see Appendix). The survey questions were designed to extract qualitative data developed through the context of the DIA model of the heart triangle. We paid particular interest inside the triangle, how they believed, loved, and became. We wanted to know what changed in their lives, and how it changed through the grieving experience. We chose to interview bereaved clients who had used our services over the past year (January 2015 to December 2015). We felt that this would control for people who have had enough time elapse from the time of death to give us an accurate picture of the results of the process. Twenty-three past clients, who received individual or family counseling from our bereavement team at Hospice of the North Coast, agreed to participate in the interview which lasted approximately one hour. Sixteen of the participants had loved ones die on our service, and seven were community clients. Community clients are defined as people receiving bereavement services from Hospice of the North Coast who's loved one did not die on our service, and may not have had hospice services. Six of the participants were male, and 17 were female. All of the participants were mature adults over age 40.

Limitations of the Findings

We found areas that can broaden our understanding of our impact in future efforts.

1. Limiting our choice of participants to only those that we helped in individual counseling may have given us a biased view of our data. In truth we are not sure how much our intervention helps versus the idea that perhaps the grieving process on its own can produce enrichment. It would be interesting to include those that suffered losses and did not receive help. By including this population we may better understand the impact of grieving on its own versus receiving professional help.

2. We did not analyze variables that would increase our understanding, such as categorizing the participants by type of loss, the length of time they grieved, age of the participant, and by normal grief and complicated grief. For example child loss is more complex and takes much longer than the other types of losses (Rando, 1984). The length of time can make a large difference as it gives time for one to adjust to the loss (Cassidy & Shaver, 2008). Age makes a different due to human development. Ones experiences, and time of life when the loss happens has an impact on the meaning of the death (Fosha, 2005) (Rando, 1984). Complicated grief is defined by its symptoms which include the following from the Mayo Clinic (Mayo Clinic Staff, 2016):

➤ Intense sorrow and pain at the thought of your loved one

➤ Focus on little else but your loved one's death

➤ Extreme focus on reminders of the loved one or excessive avoidance of reminders

➤ Intense and persistent longing or pining for the deceased

➤ Problems accepting the death

➤ Numbness or detachment

➤ Bitterness about your loss

➤ Feeling that life holds no meaning or purpose

➤ Irritability or agitation

➤ Lack of trust in others

➤ Inability to enjoy life or think back on positive experiences with your loved one

Accounting for complicated grief is essential to better understand our impact, and develop beneficial strategies to help those with multiple losses, and mental health conditions such as Major Depression, Bipolar Disorder, Schizophrenia, and the spectrum of Personality Disorders.

3. We did not categorize the therapeutic methods used in therapy. Having this information would strengthen our findings as we might have insight to what works, and what does not. There were many comments of how helpful and important the counselors were to them, but we do not have a clear idea of what interventions, if any, were used.

Findings

Finding 1: *Being Stuck*

Being stuck is a common phenomenon in grieving persons which if it lasts too long can be classified as Chronic Grief, a form of complicated grief. When the bereaved are stuck they are either unwilling or unable to move forward. All of the persons surveyed had experienced times of being stuck, where they did not think they had, or would ever improve. Two out of the 23 people interviewed continue to be stuck. Adjusting to this new life is difficult, as when they commented; "It's hard…the fridge is empty, the dog needs to go to the vet, someone needs to call and meet the plumber, and I have to go to work." They have a strong need to get their needs met which blocks them from experiencing the loss in a way that helps them overcome their need. External issues like financial issues can consume ones time and energy to the degree that they have to put grieving on hold. Comments such as "I don't have time for emotions" and "I think God hates me more because he died and left me to deal with everything", are examples of how real life issues can frustrate the grieving process.

Other areas of being stuck in grief are by feelings of guilt, shame, and regret. The feelings lead to depression, anger, apathy, and distressing and intrusive thoughts related to the loss. We heard these comments from people who experienced being stuck; "I don't think I can go on" or "I felt that something died inside of me. I was no longer a whole person." Denial also plays a key part in being stuck. Most often this presents itself as being active and busy so as not to experience the pain of the loss. Repressing the thoughts of the loved one is another form of denial, when the person can't speak of them, look at photos or come in contact with any reminder of their loved one (Rando, 1984).

Significance

Understanding where a person is stuck is crucial in helping them get unstuck. As simplistic as that sounds, it is easy for the clinician to get "stuck" with the client. Understanding where, how, and why they are stuck is the key to unlocking the mystery for them. We found the survey questions we used to be a wonderful instrument in giving the clinician clarity of the where, how and why the clients are stuck. It is then that therapeutic interventions can be instituted into the treatment plan.

Finding 2: *Type of Loss*

The type of loss is characterized by the relationship of the bereaved and the person who has died, as well as how that person died. The relationship categories are: child loss, spouse loss, loss of parents, siblings, grandparents, other family, and loss of friends. The first two listed are known to be the most difficult type of loss, and thus more challenging. For instance, the literature shows that it takes about seven years to have a semblance of recovery from child loss. Where the child's life ends, the parents grief endures as they "grow up" with the lost years of their child's growth and development (Rando, 1984).

Of the 23 people surveyed, 15 had suffered spouse loss, five had lost a parent, two suffered child loss (one of these had also lost a spouse), and one grieved the loss of a sibling. Overall, at our HNC approximately 20% of survivors are spouses, 55% lost a parent, 2% lost a child, and 13% suffered other types of loss.

How a person dies is also significant. For example a death by suicide is very troubling for the survivors, as they try to understand why, or blame themselves for not doing more (Rando, 1984). Most commonly in our experience at HNC, we are working with people who were not only related to the deceased but also provided caregiving to them, some for a prolonged period of time. This is not to imply one type of death is more or less troublesome, as reaction to loss is personal and different for each individual, but it does help to understand that survivor's experience.

Significance

By analyzing types of loss, methodologies can be implemented to help the bereaved resolve their grief. One of the methods we now use is Eye Movement Desensitization Reprocessing (EMDR), which is a technique that helps the mind to overcome troubling memories and emotions (Shapiro, 2001). Another method we use is Expressive Arts Therapy which allows the client to work through their grief non-verbally. There are two new therapies worth investigating, Accelerated Experiential Dynamic Psychotherapy (AEDP), and Induced After Death Communication (IADC).

AEDP is a technique that helps the client work through difficult emotions in which the clinician safely provides expertise in safely having them experience and work through them. By facing their emotions they make new meaning which helps resolve disturbing beliefs and builds resiliency (Fosha, 2005).

IADC or Induced After Death Communication discovered by Dr. Allan Botkin, is a method that helps resolve deep sadness. Dr. Botkins work stemmed from working with active military men and women as well as veterans suffering from PTSD. This method uses EMDR technology, but is not associated with EMDR or the EMDR Institute of America. It is similar to having a dream of your loved one and in the dream you are able to resolve your feelings of loss, guilt etc., only in this case it occurs through this therapeutic process (Botkin & Hogan, 2014).

Finding 3: *Attachment Style*

Attachment style, as defined by Fraley and Shaver (2000), is the systematic pattern of relational expectations, emotions, and behaviors that results from internalization of a particular history of attachment experiences. Attachment in this context is how one relates to others. Ones style of attachment is formed in the first two years of life, and greatly influences how you relate in your adult relationships. John Bowlby, the father of attachment theory hypothesized that the reason Charles Darwin suffered from recurrent and persistent gastric pains, nausea, and heart palpitations was due to repressed and unresolved grief from the death of his mother at age eight. He also proposed the theory that adults have the same feeling of distress and anxiety a child suffers when separated from their mother, after suffering the loss of a loved one.

We did not measure or assess the impact attachment style has on grief, but our survey revealed that those that seemed to have a secure attachment style seemed to navigate grief more productively. Those that seemed to be stuck and suffer for prolonged periods tried to get their attachment needs met without resolving their grief. For example, one spouse that was interviewed was constantly searching to replace the spouse that was lost. This person was preoccupied in replacing what they had lost, instead of reshaping their life and growing beyond their sense of need, to a sense of interdependence.

The four attachment styles are listed and explained thusly:

Secure Personality: People who formed secure attachments in childhood have secure attachment patterns in adulthood. They have a strong sense of themselves and they desire close associations with others. They basically have a positive view of themselves, their partners and their relationships. Their lives are balanced: they are both secure in their independence and in their close relationships.

Dismissive Personality: Those who had avoidant attachments in childhood most likely have dismissive attachment patterns as adults. These people tend to be loners; they regard relationships and emotions as being relatively unimportant. They are cerebral and suppress their feelings. Their typical response to conflict and stressful situations is to avoid them by distancing themselves. These people's lives are not balanced: they are inward and isolated, and emotionally removed from themselves and others.

Preoccupied Personality: Children who have an ambivalent/ anxious attachment often grow up to have preoccupied attachment patterns. As adults, they are self-critical and insecure. They seek approval and reassurance from others, yet this never relieves their self-doubt. In their relationships, deep-seated feelings that they are going to be rejected make them worried and not trusting. This drives them to act clingy and overly dependent with their partner. These people's lives are not balanced: their insecurity leaves them turned against themselves and emotionally desperate in their relationships.

Fearful-Avoidant Personality: People who grew up with disorganized attachments often develop fearful-avoidant patterns of attachment. Since, as children, they detached from their feelings during times of trauma, as adults, they continue to be somewhat detached from themselves. They desire relationships and are comfortable in them until they develop emotionally close. At this point, the feelings that were repressed in childhood begin to resurface and, with no awareness of them being from the past, they are experienced in the present. The person is no longer in life today but rather, is suddenly re-living an old trauma. These people's lives are not balanced: they do not have a coherent sense of themselves nor do they have a clear connection with others (Cassidy & Shaver, 2008).

Significance

Bowlby stated that those with poor attachment styles will likely suffer from psychological and physical distress following a loss. Assessing a person's attachment style and hyperactivating their attachment can assist the survivor in exploring and making new meaning of their loss, and thus can reorganize their bond with their loved one in a productive fashion (Cassidy & Shaver, 2008). Expressive Arts Therapy, EMDR, and AEDP, can be useful interventions to assist with this process.

Finding 4: *Resiliency*

Resiliency is defined as the ability to become strong, healthy, or successful again after something bad happens; or the ability of something to return to its original shape after it has been pulled, stretched, pressed, or bent (APA, July, 2016). Grief itself has been described by our clients in just this fashion. The comments we noted bear this out. "I was shattered"; "I felt like I was being pulled apart"; or "I haven't made any effort". When the team discussed the data, we asked; "what caused the changes they were sharing?" We were curious what made them enriched through the process, yet others were struggling. When we discussed each person we realized that resiliency seemed to play a large part in the results of grieving, and as we discussed further we learned that those that seemed to demonstrate high resiliency in their past, had better outcomes with their grief. It thus became important that we find a way to measure resiliency, and learn how to help people develop it. Resiliency is directly related to our impact 'The bereaved will be enriched through the grieving experience' as was demonstrated in the comments of those that felt enriched. Comments like; "I am active"(I care for myself), "I now believe I did the right thing"(I am confident), "I now believe in my own abilities"(I am confident), and "I was afraid of what grief could be, but now I love the opportunities I have"(I am confident & hopeful). These statements demonstrate key components to resilience. They demonstrate that they are reaching out and making connections, overcoming difficult issues, and difficult emotions. They also demonstrate self-care, and active pursuit of self-growth. These are all components of building resilience (APA, July, 2016).

Significance

Resilience can be measured and improved. The measurement scales that have been tested vary as to reliability and validity. Recent studies have identified three scales that rate better than the rest; they are: the Connor-Davidson Resilience Scale and the Resilience Scale for Adults and the Brief Resilience Scale received the best psychometric ratings (Windle, Bennett, & Noyes, 2011). These scales can be used to measure each client's resiliency, so that interventions can be instituted that would build resiliency and increase the possibility that the client is enriched by the grieving process.

Finding 5: *Grief is Trauma*

The American Psychological Association defines trauma as: "an emotional response to a terrible event like an accident, rape or natural disaster. Immediately after the event, shock and denial are typical. Longer term reactions include unpredictable emotions, flashbacks, strained relationships and even physical symptoms like headaches or nausea. While these feelings are normal, some people have difficulty moving on with their lives. Psychologists can help these individuals find constructive ways of managing their emotions" (Trauma, 2016). Of the 23 people interviewed, 14 expressed trauma related comments. Such as: "I think of how they died, and that I couldn't do anything", "I wasn't sure I made the right decisions", "I can see the helpless look on their face", and "I have difficult images of my wife at death".

Death is uncommon and foreign to the large majority in this country. It makes us feel uncomfortable to be near, and can be traumatizing to watch someone die (Rando, 1984).

Significance

There are therapeutic interventions that have very good efficacy for trauma (Shapiro, 2001). EMDR, is currently being used in our agency with positive results. Seven of the clients interviewed had EMDR treatment; all had positive outcomes of reducing the trauma of their experience. Another intervention we use is Expressive Arts Therapy, which has less talking and enables the client to work through their trauma non-verbally. It is unknown what modalities of therapy respondents had at the time of therapy.

Finding 6: *Bereaved are Enriched*

We found that 13 of the 23 people interviewed were enriched through their process. Six were improved, and four were stuck. Enrichment was measured by the clients stating they had higher purpose, that their grief was resolved, they were grateful for what they gained in the process, and that they loved their lives, but I will let those that were enriched speak for themselves and let us listen to the message inside the triangle of, "I believe", "I became", and "I Love".

"I felt guilty about the decisions I made because they upset my mother, but they had to be done. I now believe I did the right thing."

"I've become liberated!"

"I feel recovered from grief"

"I now believe in my own abilities, and believe life can and will be full."

"I can move forward in life and have purpose"

"I am engaging with my children and I'm finding a deeper connection with them."

"I know life has more purpose."

"I learned I had a choice...move forward or feel sorry for myself. I chose moving forward."

"I've become grateful; I love others that hurt me."

"I am expressing myself with words and art!"

"I am comfortable in my own skin."

"I learned to believe in my instincts and to act on them"

"I want to be a kinder, softer, and gentler person. This desire opened up for me through this process."

"I believe I can live a hopeful and enriched life."

"I'm confident I can handle life and make the right decisions."

"I have a lot more confidence now than I have before in my life."

"I know there is a future for me."

It is inspiring that out of great pain and suffering, there is enrichment and a life worth living. These people made a choice to lean into the pain and to learn about themselves, and to take those lessons into a new way of perceiving and living life. We all have that choice.

Significance

Our findings are encouraging that people are enriched through the grieving experience. It's not clear however how much counseling contributes, or how much the process itself is enriching. However, the comments the respondents had about their counselors suggests that they felt they were very helpful in assisting them to navigate through the grief process. Just knowing that the grieving process can lead one to feel enriched can be a boost to the spirits, hope, and confidence of both the clinician and the bereaved.

Implications and Actions

This process has broadened and deepened our understanding of the grieving process and our commitment to assist those who are on that journey. Because of this understanding we have identified strategies to strengthen and improve our bereavement program. The following are strategies we intend to implement:

1. **Snap Shot:** This is to continue to use our survey questions to take a "snap shot" of the bereaved client's progress intermittently in the process. This process showed us clearly how the respondents had progressed, and where they became stuck.

2. **Training:** We feel it is important to be at the forefront of new therapies and ideas that are researched, and efficacious. Two have been mentioned in our findings, AEDP, and IADC. EMDR has been endorsed by our team and adopted into our program.

3. **New Assessments:** We will begin assessing for attachment styles, resiliency, and trauma to help us understand the clients resources, and to initiate appropriate interventions to help with difficult attachment, build resilience, and to directly treat trauma.

Venice Family Clinic

Homeless Services Program

Karen Lauterbach

Stephanie Stilling

Ryan Woodson, MPH

Acknowledgement

First and foremost, we would like to thank the Gumpert Foundation and the Project Impact team. The Gumpert Foundation's generosity made this experience possible for Venice Family Clinic. It's wonderful to know funders that believe in offering capacity-building experiences to non-profits. Thank you, Gumpert Foundation, for inviting VFC into this Project Impact cohort. Also, we are happy that Venice Family Clinic gave us the time and space to have this experience, allowing us to learn more about hour homeless program and develop recommendations to strengthen it. Next, Steve and Jess, you were our fearless Project Impact leaders on this program evaluation journey. Thank you both for being such dynamic and thoughtful facilitators. We appreciate the support and guidance you gave us along the way.

We wish to acknowledge the Venice Family Clinic staff who gave us their time and feedback on our interviews and surveys. We were so lucky to have a cadre of talented and dedicated VFC volunteers to help us interview and survey patients. This included Christine Sutanto, Denisse Ruiz and Carla del Cid. We also want to thank two partner organizations – OPCC and Safe Place for Youth (SPY) – for helping us recruit patients for this project and giving us access to meeting space. And, of course, thank you SO MUCH to the dozens of VFC patients who gave us their time and shared their VFC experience with us. We are grateful for your openness and candor; thank you for sharing your personal stories with us. We learned so much from you all.

Most sincerely,

Karen, Stephanie, and Ryan

Executive Summary

Venice Family Clinic (VFC) is the primary provider of comprehensive healthcare and social services to homeless individuals and families on the Westside of Los Angeles County in LA County Service Planning Area (SPA) 5. Founded in response to the grave prevalence of homelessness on the Westside of Los Angeles, Venice Family Clinic's Homeless Services Program aims to improve the health and wellbeing of homeless men, women and children. Just last year, VFC provided quality medical, dental, mental health, health insurance and other services to over 3,000 homeless individual and families.

This report is an evaluation of VFC's Homeless Services Program. The goal of the evaluation is to identify and illustrate the impact of VFC's Homeless Program in the health and wellness of our homeless patients. We intend on using the data to inform and enhance our homeless services to best fit the direct health and social needs of the homeless individuals and families that call Venice Family Clinic home.

Key Findings

We found that our homeless patients are on a trajectory to better health. The findings below summarize our patient's trajectory and VFC's role in their path to progress.

Home sweet home: VFC is viewed as a home for our homeless patients, with welcoming staff and comprehensive services that transcends medical care.

Health in command: VFC is helping homeless patients take control of their lives by improving their health.

Speaking up and being heard: Strong patient-provider relationships are giving homeless patients a voice and a supportive forum to be heard.

Sharing the health wealth: Homeless patients embody their health successes by passing them along to others.

Walk beside me: VFC partners with and supports patients; we instill hope in our patients and help them identify their path to good health and ultimately reach their goals.

You are what you eat (and drink): Homeless patients' lives are extremely complicated, and yet, they still continue to prioritize eating well and exercise.

Learning in action: Homeless patients and their health improve as they put into action what they learn about exercise, physical therapy and medication management.

Recommendations

Our recommendations consist of strategies that aim to support and empower our homeless patients on their path to becoming the healthiest versions of themselves.

Introduction to Venice Family Clinic

Founded in 1970, the mission of Venice Family Clinic (VFC) is to provide quality primary health care to people in need. VFC first operated in a small, storefront dental office after normal business hours. Over the decades we've grown to 10 health centers in Venice, Santa Monica, Mar Vista and Culver City. There was—and remains—a tremendous unmet need for affordable health care on the Westside of Los Angeles for those who live in poverty. In our growth, we strive to meet patients where they live, work or go to school.

Today, VFC's core programs are medical, dental and vision care, mental health, chronic disease management, prenatal care, early childhood development, health education and wellness, health insurance enrollment, case management, and lab and pharmacy operations. With 252 staff members and 733 physician volunteers, we currently serve over 22,000 unique patients in more than 103,000 visits each year. The pie graphs below summarize the demographics of Venice Family Clinic's current patient population.

Figure 1. Venice Clinic Family Patient Demographics

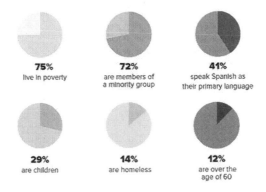

75%	**72%**	**41%**
live in poverty	are members of a minority group	speak Spanish as their primary language
29%	**14%**	**12%**
are children	are homeless	are over the age of 60

Program Description

Venice Family Clinic (VFC) is the primary provider of comprehensive health care to homeless residents on the Westside of Los Angeles in LA County Service Planning Area (SPA) 5, as shown in the map below. VFC serves as the medical home for 3,000 homeless men, women and children each year.

There is a tremendous unmet need for health care, social services and resources for homeless individuals in LA County. Of the 56,000 homeless in LA County, SPA 5 has about 4,600 homeless individuals or 10% of the County's total. Also, in the past year alone, SPA 5 experienced a 9% increase in homelessness while some other SPAs saw decreases

Program Activities

To address the needs of local homeless individuals, Venice Family Clinic's provides a comprehensive primary care services programs along with a wide range of complementary supportive services. Our full menu of homeless services includes:

- ➤ Primary care including diagnoses, treatments, laboratory tests and medications.
- ➤ Specialty care such as dermatology, neurology, rheumatology and more.
- ➤ Chronic disease management for issues like asthma, cardiovascular disease and diabetes.
- ➤ Vision care services such as ophthalmology, optometry and digital retinal screening.
- ➤ Dental services including cleanings, tooth extractions, x-rays, root canals and fillings.
- ➤ Behavioral health services including counseling, support groups, case management and medication.
- ➤ Substance use treatment.
- ➤ Integrated mobile health to triage and care for homeless patients where they live.
- ➤ Specialized services to meet the needs of homeless youth, teens, and families.
- ➤ Health education for chronic disease prevention and management.
- ➤ Assistance finding supportive housing and other needed services.

VFC proactively addresses the health care needs of the Westside's homeless population through our health centers, satellite locations, street teams and unique partnership programs including:

VFC Health Centers – Five VFC health centers located in Venice, Santa Monica and Mar Vista provide accessible medical care to homeless patients through walk-in hours, ensuring they are seen with or without an appointment. Access to showers, toiletries, and clean clothing ensures everyone seeing a physician at VFC does so with dignity and respect. Patients may also engage with mental health services, substance abuse counseling, and health education. Dental care is also available at our dental suite in Santa Monica, including transportation from another clinic or the beach community.

Integrated Mobile Health Team (IMHT – VFC Outreach): Provides health care to homeless individuals who are unable or unwilling to access services at one of our clinics. Using a registry that has identified the highest need population, a team of medical providers from VFC, along with case managers and other support staff from partner organizations visit clients where they live to provide medical care and supportive services including housing.

Common Ground: Part of VFC, this program provides a drop in center for HIV-positive individuals Monday through Friday, where almost half of the clients are homeless. Targeted care provides much needed support for our most vulnerable patient's case management benefits specific to HIV mental health and drop in, support groups, partner services and syringe exchange. Patients have access to the internet, phone, food, storage within a home like setting. Case managers work closely with clients to ensure is the link to their medical provider for the appropriate management of their HIV.

Ocean Park Community Center (OPCC): Provides care to homeless individuals at OPCC's Access Center five days a week. This includes comprehensive medical care, lab, vaccinations, nursing and close coordination with OPCC case management team. This site serves clients from the Access Center, OPCC shelters and the respite program.

Safe Place for Youth (SPY): Provides medical and dental care to homeless youth twice a week on-site at SPY's drop-in center. Because young homeless individuals are distrustful and unwilling to engage with most service providers, VFC's satellite clinic provides medical care and a safe entry point for youth to begin accessing VFC services at our locations in Venice and Santa Monica.

Venice Chronic Homeless Intervention Project (V-CHIP): Once a week, at the St. Joseph's Homeless Access Center, we provide medical services to their clients with the highest need. This is to provide services where clients are most comfortable and are connected to case management and housing support services.

Intended Impact

There are two key direct impacts we intend to have on our homeless patients.

1. **Homeless are engaged in their health.** Homeless work in concert with their health care team to set and achieve their health goals.

   The measurable indicators associated with this first impact are: 1a) Homeless embrace their personal health trajectory; and, 1b) Homeless embody hope about their health.

2. **Homeless lead healthier lives.** Homeless become the healthiest version of themselves.

   The measurable indicators associated with our second impact are: 2a) Homeless are dedicated to their health; 2b) Homeless become the healthiest version of themselves; and, 2c) Homeless become advocates for health.

Homeless patients come to Venice Family Clinic. From there they can access any or all of the myriad services available to them. With their active participation and support of VFC staff and volunteers, our homeless patients' health improves over time.

Further, we expect our impact on homeless patients to have a ripple effect to improve other aspects of their lives as well as the larger homeless population on the Westside of Los Angeles. These additional direct and indirect impacts include:

> ➤ Direct: Homeless become advocates for themselves.

> ➤ Secondary: Homeless lead more stable lives.

Tertiary: Homeless on the Westside of Los Angeles have improved access to health and social services.

Methodology

VFC serves 3,100 homeless patients annually. Representing 14% of our total patient population, homeless patients are deemed a priority because of the unique and complex socio-economic challenges they experience. Because these challenges directly influence their access and utilization of health care services, this mixed-methods evaluation is an essential first step in determining the impact of VFC's Homeless Services Program.

Study Design

This mixed-methods evaluation aimed to understand the impact of VFC's Homeless Services Program in the health and wellness of homeless patients. We designed an in-depth interview protocol using the Heart Triangle method of question construction. This produced a protocol that consisted of nine sequences of questions (18 questions in total). The protocol was used as a guide for data collection. It allowed us to capture the interviewee's awareness and reflection of structural shifts, and development of growth and progress. We also designed a quantitative questionnaire to collect data on specific indicators of impact. We administered the quantitative survey electronically to 63 homeless patients. The quantitative data were analyzed using measures of central tendency.

Over the course of seven months, we (a) developed and refined our ideas of intended impact and indicators, (b) designed and implemented qualitative (in-depth interviews) and quantitative research (questionnaires) tools for data collection, (c) conducted 16 in-depth interviews and 63 questionnaires, and (d) analyzed the data and identified key findings. Lastly, we will use the findings and their respective implications to develop strategies to inform health and social programming for homeless patients.

Study Population and Sample Size

We identified a sample of subject using a purposeful stratified technique to select a representation of the total homeless population we serve. Our sample size for the in-depth interviews consisted of 16 homeless patients with varying housing status and points in care. It was drawn to ensure a balanced representation of the diverseness of our homeless patient population. Our sample size for the quantitative surveys consisted of 63 patients with varying housing status and points in care. The specific characteristics of the study participants are shown below in Tables 1 and 2. The primary exclusion criterion was point in care.

New patients, defined as those patients who have been a VFC patient for less than six months and patients with less than a total of four visits (including medical, dental, behavioral health, and health insurance), were excluded.

Table 1: In-depth Interviews (IDI) and Questionnaires Participants by Housing Status

	Street Up	Doubling	Shelter Housed	Newly	Total
IDI	7	2	4	2	16
SurveyMonkey Survey	33	6	16	8	63

Table 2: In-depth Interviews (IDI) and Questionnaires Participants by Point in Care

	6 Months	6 Months to 1 Year	1-3 Years	3 Years <	Total
IDI	5	4	5	2	16
SurveyMonkey Survey	18	9	13	23	63

Data Collection and Analysis

We conducted 16 in-depth qualitative interviews lasting between 45 and 60 minutes in length, and 63 quantitative questionnaires. Qualitative data were collected via notes during the interview, and then augmented immediately following the interview to provide a substantive rendering of the interview. Quantitative data were collected electronically and via manual data entry via SurveyMonkey.

We applied a four-step model of textual analysis to each of the interviews. This process allowed us to interpret the meaning and significance of the interview data. The quantitative data were analyzed via SurveyMonkey.

Results

The overarching themes that emerged from the data were identified and examined to illuminate primary insights and discoveries. Our evaluation yielded findings that captured the primary discoveries from the data. The most salient of the findings are described in the following narrative.

Findings

Finding 1: *"Home Sweet Home"*

Venice Family Clinic (VFC) is a medical home to over 3,100 homeless individuals and families on the Westside of Los Angeles. Our Homeless Services Program is tailored to provide a wide array of primary, specialty, and other healthcare-related services, like health insurance enrollment, to meet homeless patients wherever they may be, physically and mentally. Homeless patients reported feeling extremely cared for, supported, and respected by VFC. As the name suggests, Venice Family was often described as a home, with a welcoming staff that treats homeless patients with compassion, dignity and respect. Staff were described as friendly sources of support, who connected patients to the services they needed. When describing his interactions with one of VFC's front desk staff, a patient said:

"The chronic pain coordinator is excellent. It is very thorough and it feels just like family."

VFC was described as a safe and welcoming place that provided comfort and care to patients when they needed it the most. Given their challenging circumstances, patients often reported feeling lonely, isolated, and without support until they became patients of VFC. One patient described VFC as a place that provided her not only with healthcare, but also emotional support that made her feel acknowledged, respected and appreciated.

"When I was homeless, VFC was the only place that showed me kindness. And sometimes, that was the only kindness I'd received in days."

When asked how VFC has helped her, another patient said:

"Even though I lived very far away now, I still come to VFC because I am so faithful to the services I've gotten here in a time when I was all alone."

Significance

This finding is particularly significant because it shows that VFC's impact in the lives of our homeless patients transcends health outcomes. VFC's services, staff and providers are providing a sense of security for patients without stability in one or more aspects of their lives. VFC's team is helping homeless patients feel better about themselves by welcoming them into a space in which they are treated with respect, dignity and compassion. Because of the services provided by VFC, homeless patients mobilized to be the healthiest version of themselves.

Our Response

VFC uses two training modules to address patient communication and the needs of our homeless patients: Trauma-informed care and CICARE, a set of six communication behaviors to guide the best possible interactions with everyone on every encounter. Based on our findings, patients experience positive interactions with staff, which make them feel comfortable at VFC; therefore, we recommend continued trauma-informed care and CICARE training for existing staff and all new hires with an enhanced emphasis on culturally-sensitive and appropriate techniques for homeless patients.

Finding 2: *"Health in Command"*

The inability to control many factors in the life of our patients was an omnipresent theme. Patients reported feeling unable to control essential needs, such as food, housing, employment, transportation, appearance and personal possessions. However, after becoming a VFC patient the salient health challenged they once faced were now more in their command. Patients were very proud of the progress they made tackling their health issues and they often stated that their past health challenges are now sources of empowerment and motivation to fuel improvements in other aspects of their lives. When asked about how he has changed since becoming a patient of VFC, one patient stated:

> "I take my health more seriously. I feel more in control of my diabetes and it feels good … taking more responsibility for my health, I mean."

The personal satisfaction patients received in overcoming their health challenges, often positively impacted their interpersonal relationships with family members and friends. When asked if friends or family see her differently, one patient replied:

> "My daughter sees me differently, in a more positive way since I've started dealing with and fixing my addiction … I am encouraged to continue reflecting on what I can change."

Furthermore, the personal satisfaction patients received in overcoming their health challenges impacted how they felt about their place in society and in the workforce. For example, when asked about how her outlook on life has changed, since becoming a patient of VFC, one patient said:

> "Now that my pain is managed, I feel in control. I am motivated to start looking for a job."

Significance

The salient challenges of being homeless continued to emerged throughout the interviews. In the survey, when asked if "after VFC, I feel more capable of taking care of my health", 78% responded with a "strongly agree" or "agree", as referenced in the chart below. While significant barriers will continue in the lives of our patients, our care provides them with the support they need to take charge.

After VFC, I feel more more capable of taking care of myself

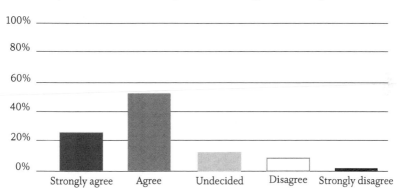

Our Response

Our patients provide a lot of insight to their services and needs. We should capitalize on this and systemize their input through a regular patient advisory meeting and/or quarterly surveys. This should include review of materials and teaching tools are culturally-appropriate and tailored to our homeless population. This increased involvement will ideally lead to additional skill sets.

Finding 3: *"Speaking up and Being Heard"*

In-depth interviews revealed that our homeless patients feel silenced by society. This sentiment directly impacted their health, wellbeing and feelings of self-worth. When speaking about the specific challenges he faces, one patient stated:

> "Because I am homeless, I feel doubted, like I am taking advantage. But what you don't understand is that little things to you are a big problem for me..."

Homelessness and health care are connected. With higher incidences of mental health issues, chronic conditions, and ultimately a shorter life expectancy: between 42-52 years, compared to 78 years in the general population (http://www.nationalhomeless.org/factsheets/health.html), it is imperative that our homeless patients feel comfortable sharing their issues and more importantly, confident that they will be heard. While these findings were sobering, we learned from further analysis that VFC providers are building strong patient-provider relationships that are instilling confidence and empowering homeless patients to speak up, without a fear of being ignored. As a result, VFC providers are positively impacting homeless patients' health, well-being and feeling of self-worth through communication and compassion.

> "This place is full compassion and doctors who care about opinions and want to take care of you."

Patients reported that their provider understands them, cares for them and ultimately, respects them. This made patients feel respected, encouraged and empowered to make important changes to improve their health. When describing her relationship with her provider, one patient stated:

> "I can be honest about my health with my doctor and because of that I feel more empowered and confident in taking care of myself."

Additionally, the acknowledgement and collaboration provided to patients by their provider was often described as the guiding force behind a patient's motivation to get better. When asked how her health has improved since becoming a patient of VFC, she stated:

> "When I started at the clinic I used multiple times a week, then I started to slowly decrease to once a week. And now I haven't used in about 4 weeks. I really appreciate Dr. Chung for helping me.... he is very professional and treats me with respect."

Significance

This finding is particularly significant because it shows that VFC's providers are directly impacting the lives of our homeless patients in a way that transcends health. They are instilling confidence, trust, and empowerment in patients that are undoubtable in the most need. Because of the compassion provided by VFC physician, homeless patients are mobilized to be the healthiest and honest version of themselves.

Our Response

VFC providers and staff already do a terrific job of making homeless patients feel welcome, supported and comfortable at our locations. Our hope is that this report has illuminated the provider- patient relationships that exist at VFC; by reading this report, providers will gain a greater understanding of and take pride in their positive impact on our homeless population. We recommend continuous training for all providers and staff in ways to further instill confidence, trust and empowerment in our patients.

Finding 4: *"Sharing the health wealth"*

Our homeless patients showed a tremendous sense of motivation and responsibility related to taking care of themselves and their health. They talked about taking pride in tackling certain health challenges they've faced. In some cases, patients learned so much from VFC that they felt compelled to share this information with friends or family members. Based on our survey results, 79% strongly agreed/agreed that after coming to VFC "my health knowledge has increased". This was one of our ultimate hopes for VFC's homeless health care program – homeless patients would become advocates for health. Thanks to our patient Bonny, her son is also now a VFC patient and gets the care he needs. She tells us she never hesitates to "refer new people all the time." She is proud to share that she beat cervical cancer! People in her life look at her as a true role model who spreads "encouraging words to everyone." She tries her best to "lead by example" and healthy habits are one of the most important aspects. Our interviews confirmed that our most powerful recruitment tool is patient referrals. Patients like Bonny who have experienced healing and positive gains at Venice Family Clinic are motivated to share information about VFC with their friends and family.

Significance

Our homeless patients remarked that their friends and family members have noticed the positive changes they were making as well as their improved attitudes and outlooks. Improvements in someone's health have the ability to impact other areas of their lives, including behaviors, lifestyle choices and even personal relationships. T.M. reflects that her daughter sees her"Differently and in a positive way since I started looking at my addiction and coming off Benzos."

Since becoming a VFC patient Jason "reached out to reconnect with my father." He's a health advocate for his father and does "encourage him to take better care of himself, too." Jason leads by example and works hard to continue to cut back on drinking alcohol. These patients benefit from the care they receive at VFC and are excited to share this information with the people in their lives who also have health concerns. The health education information Michael has received has made a big impact on his life. He says, "VFC has helped me take my role in my health more seriously. I want to take responsibility for my health."

Patients reported feeling encouraged to share health knowledge and other information about VFC with others in need. VFC is a trusted resource they feel comfortable sharing with their loved ones. Jeffrey shares,"My friends have noticed that I look happier and healthier. I feel more stable emotionally and know I'm in good hands at VFC."

Our Response

VFC must continue to encourage homeless patients to share their health knowledge and information about VFC with their friends and families. Use the Common Ground model of support groups and educational classes and evaluate how this could be used clinic wide as a means of empowerment and support. We will identify ways to clearly and intentionally address these topics with patients and empower them to become health advocates for themselves and in their communities/networks.

Finding 5: *"Walk beside me"*

Homeless patients face a number of challenges and complexities in their everyday lives that make this a unique and needy population at Venice Family Clinic – housing instability or lack of housing, street dangers, substance use, stigmas related to being homeless, unable to have appropriate hygiene or personal appearance, and, of course, unaddressed health concerns. They each have a unique health trajectory that VFC is participating in a positive way and our services are meeting them where they are at. On the day of Thomas' interview, it was the first day he had seen himself in the mirror in a week. He was missing a tooth and had a huge cut on his head that was unexplained. He talked about being overwhelmed by everything but knew he needed "to do something." Coming to VFC was his first step because he "needed to get things started."

R.C. talked about how "some days my mind still stops me from taking showers and I am not motivated to take care of myself, but there are good days as well."

Some were able to move on to focus on healing. X said, "My goal is lower by blood pressure…I will not always have one hundred percent relief days but at least I have the tools to attempt to make my day better".

Jeffrey talked about an injury he has and that, "I have received more attention than I have had in my life. I have been given good advice on how to care for it (shoulder)and not injure it further even though I am on the streets."

Through the care received at VFC, patients relayed a sense of hope and optimism for their futures. T.M. admits, "it's a long road to become healthy, and I hope to see it someday." She hopes to maintain the "progress I've made with VFC's help."

As a result of his improved health, Jason appreciates "life more and doesn't want to die."

When asked about his future health Frank said, "I am excited to continue my path unless my doctors tell me otherwise. I am excited to look forward and see what God has next. All will fall into the right place."

Significance

Patients see VFC as a place to move forward on their journey to better health. Our survey showed that 60% strongly agreed or agreed that they worried less about their health since receiving services at VFC. Thomas, who has been our patient for four years illustrated this best; at a low point in life, he looked to us to help get back on track. Jeffery has surgery scheduled for his shoulder and feels like this will put him on the path to employment.

Our Response

VFC will maintain our collaboration with local organizations focused on housing assistance, financial literacy, job training/placement and more. We should continue to evaluate how we can be involved at a policy level to ensure that the needs of our patients continue to be heard and met. These services are critically needed by our homeless patients and VFC will continue to refer patients to these organizations and/or invite organizations to deliver these trainings and services on-site at an existing VFC location.

Finding 6: *"You are what you eat (and drink)."*

Struggling with access to enough food is a common stereotype of people living on the street. Therefore, it was not surprising that access to food and water was a persistent theme in the interviews. However, the issue was not a simple matter of not being able to get enough to eat. Patients made the connection between their diet and their health, believing that an improvement to their nutrition would improve their overall health. When asked about what changes they have made in their health here are some of the responses:

"I am more aware of what goes into my body. I'd rather have stevia than sugar and eat more vegetables."

"Nutrition is my major change. I eat in the morning now and am making better food choices"

Many referred to their healthy habits as a source of pride:

"I am most proud that I lost a lot of weight through healthy eating and exercise" Jeffrey reports "eating healthier, choosing to live clean – free of drugs and alcohol"

They also made the connection to their specific health condition. Many mentioned eating better and drinking more water for ailments such as diabetes, Hepatitis C, liver disease and high blood pressure. Many made a further connection of reducing or stopping alcohol to help with their health condition.

When talking about skills they have to manage their health, diet is often mentioned. One patient talked about going to the food bank on top of her food stamps so she can "still get the healthy foods she needs to eat for her health".

At the same time, frustration was expressed at having little control over their food and water. R.C. talked about this challenge around drinking water,"It is too heavy to carry a lot but I need it to take meds. Many places charge for water so I have to know where all of the fountains are so I can get water throughout the day." A.K., a diabetic patient, said he wants to eat the right way "but can't because shelters give him whatever"and the Clinic "they just gave me a list of things I can't really afford". He went on to say that "[f]ood (distributions) is usually just one meal so you try to go to many places but they serve at the same time, you try to get extra so you have food for the next day. You are always searching for food."

Ricky indicates that he's "struggling to find healthier food alternatives." VFC has made him more aware of the need to eat healthy and this knowledge, in part, keeps him motivated to continue to be proactive about accessing healthy foods.

Significance

It was encouraging to learn that many patients prioritize their health in these ways and to hear patients talk about trying to choose healthy foods, when the assumption could be that they would be happy to take any food they could get. Our patients believe in the connection between their nutrition and their health. In the survey, when asked what changes in their health they are making as a result of what they learned at VFC we expected answers around their specific health condition. However, 38% specifically named diet and hydration as the change they were making. We have a tremendous opportunity to augment our support to help with these health goals.

Our Response

Since so many of homeless patients showed a commitment to eating healthier, there are ways in which VFC must better assist them with diet and nutrition. VFC can help identify healthy and organic food and beverage resources on the Westside. Homeless patients' limited or non-existent food budgets prevent them from accessing healthy, unprocessed foods. VFC may consider seeking out dedicated private funding or corporate donations to ease this burden for our homeless patients. VFC can also revisit its current grocery gift store and determine ways to expand or adjust it to better meet the need and/or reach additional homeless patients. Lastly, we can provide information on how to maximize food stamps, when applicable. For instance, many farmers' markets will double the value of the stamps to purchase fresh fruit and vegetables. Additionally, much like we make a hot shower a part of their visit, VFC should also allow homeless patients to replenish their water supply. VFC should consider setting up water filling stations at its locations and offering patients reusable water bottles

Finding #7: *"Learning in Action"*

VFC aims to provide all patients with health education and practical advice/tools they need to manage their health after the appointment. The patients we interviewed told us about their successes and challenges with taking their medication, exercising, physical therapy and infection avoidance.

Ricky notes that he's "learned the importance of taking his medication more regularly. I have good days and bad days."

Ed talks about exercises the provider gave him for pain and he had done them "even though they make me look like a sissy."

Daphne, who was recently housed and suffers from arthritis, found a low cost place to do aquatic exercise on the advice of her provider.

Many patients mentioned different tools, e.g., pill boxes with instructions they understand, that help take their medications correctly. They also talked about different ways to keep personal hygiene up, avoid germs when living on the street and avoid prevalent skin infections. Furthermore, as indicated by the chart below, the majority of patients agreed or strongly agreed that VFC provided them with essential tools to help them care for themselves.

VFC has provided me with helpful tools to care for my health

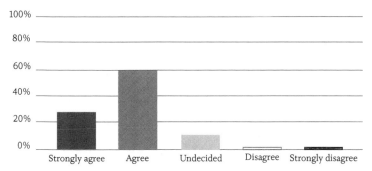

Significance

Homeless patients often present with extremely complex medical situations that would overwhelm most people. Our patients embraced the tools they were given by VFC to assist them in leading a more health filled life. Our survey showed that a resounding 87% either strongly agreed or agreed that VFC "has provided me with helpful tools to care for my health". This helps complete the picture of providing quality care in addition to the tools to continue the path of improved health.

Our Response

One way in which we can better support homeless patients on their journey to better health is to have our homeless patients help review diet and exercise health education materials; this will ensure that they are culturally-appropriate for those with unstable housing and limited budgets. All health education materials and care plans must be tailored to our homeless populations with limited resources.

Recommendations and Next Steps

The following is the author's' list of recommendations for Venice Family Clinic to improve its Homeless Services Program based on our seven findings above.

Recommendation 1: We recommend that VFC continue to incorporate CICARE and Trauma-Informed Care techniques into all of our work with homeless patients, and ensure that all staff and new hires receive these trainings. (Finding 1)

Recommendation 2: Our patients provide a lot of insight to their services and needs. We should capitalize on this and systemize their input through a regular patient advisory meeting and/or quarterly surveys. This should include review of materials and teaching tools are culturally-appropriate and tailored to our homeless population. This increased involvement will ideally lead to additional skill sets. (Finding 2)

Recommendation 3: VFC will maintain our collaboration with local organizations focused on housing assistance, financial literacy, job training/placement and more. We should continue to evaluate how we can be involved at a policy level to ensure that the needs of our patients continue to be heard and met. These services are critically needed by our homeless patients and VFC will continue to refer patients to these organizations and/or invite organizations to deliver these trainings and services on-site at an existing VFC location. (Finding 5)

Recommendation 4: VFC providers and staff already do a terrific job of making homeless patients feel welcome, supported and comfortable at our locations. Our hope is that this report has illuminated the provider-patient relationships that exist at VFC; by reading this report, providers will gain a greater understanding of and take pride in their positive impact on our homeless population. We recommend continuous training for all providers and staff in ways to further instill confidence, trust and empowerment in our patients. (Finding 3)

Recommendation 5: VFC must continue to encourage homeless patients to share their health knowledge and information about VFC with their friends and families. This will allow VFC to reach additional individuals in need of health care services. We will identify ways to clearly and intentionally address these topics with patients and empower them to become health advocates for themselves and in their communities/networks. (Finding 4)

Recommendation 6: Since so many of homeless patients showed a commitment to eating healthier, there are ways in which VFC must better assist them with diet and nutrition. VFC can help identify healthy and organic food and beverage resources on the Westside. Homeless patients' limited or non-existent food budgets prevent them from accessing healthy, unprocessed foods. VFC may consider seeking out dedicated private funding or corporate donations to ease this burden for our homeless patients. VFC can also revisit its current grocery gift store and determine ways to expand or adjust it to better meet the need and/or reach additional homeless patients. Lastly, we can provide information on how to maximize food stamps, when applicable. For instance, many farmers' markets will double the value of the stamps to purchase fresh fruit and vegetables. (Finding 6)

Recommendation 7: One way in which we can better support homeless patients on their journey to better health is to have our homeless patients help review diet and exercise health education materials; this will ensure that they are culturally-appropriate for those with unstable housing and limited budgets. All health education materials and care plans must be tailored to our homeless populations with limited resources. (Finding 7)

Recommendation 8: Much like we make a hot shower a part of their visit, VFC should also allow homeless patients to replenish their water supply. VFC should consider setting up water filling stations at its locations and offering patients reusable water bottles. (Finding 6)

SUPPORT THE ENLISTED PROJECT

Support the Enlisted Project

Emergency Financial Assistance Program

Tony Teravainen
Co-founder and President/CEO

Kathi Bradshaw
Vice President and Director of Client Services

Erica Bender
Volunteer and Ph.D. Candidate at UC San Diego

From January 2016 through August 2016, Support the Enlisted Project (STEP) participated in a multi-phase research workshop called Project Impact. The eight-month program offered training in innovative data collection techniques specifically calibrated for non-profit and community-based organizations. STEP and the Project Impact team worked closely and collaboratively to develop a comprehensive research program to assess the quality of the impact we are having for our clients and their families and communities. This report summarizes our efforts and outlines our main findings.

Acknowledgement

Our team worked hard to make this research project a success, but we would not have been able to capitalize on these efforts if it weren't for the hard work and generosity of many others. Specifically, we would like to thank:

The Gumpert Foundation, The Leichtag Foundation, Shelby Ross, Steve McClelland, STEP Board of Directors, and STEP's former clients who agreed to be interviewed and/or returned our questionnaire. We would also like to thank Steve Patty and Jessamyn Luiz for their support and guidance through this process.

Introduction to STEP

Support The Enlisted Project (STEP) assists junior active duty enlisted members and recently discharged enlisted veterans and their families in Southern California facing financial crisis achieve long term financial self-sufficiency through counseling, education and grants to alleviate critical near term obligations. STEP provides its services to the lower six paygrades (E1-E6) of our military and veterans within the first 18 months after their honorable discharge. Southern California is home to 95,000 active duty military in the E1-E6 pay grades, of which half have families. 60% of these military members are Low Income per HUD Standards; 30% rely on food assistance regularly to feed their families; 73% are under age 26. These families are also without the support systems of their hometowns as they were sent to Southern California by the military.

STEP's primary goal is to prevent these young military and veteran families from loosing one of their basic life necessities due to an accute financial crisis, and to build them towards a path of financial self-sufficiency. Everything STEP does works toward this sigular, critical goal. STEP provides emergency financial counseling and education in a one-on-one forum with a case worker who is also a social worker. This counseling and education has a goal to empower each client to take ownership of their finances, produce a monthly budget that works for their unique situation, and to produce a long-term debt reduction plan. When necessary, STEP will also provide a grant, not a loan, that will prevent the loss of the family's basic needs while the family gets back on their feet. Additionally, STEP maintains a warehouse where families can visit and pick up donated goods, such as baby supplies and home goods, and offers cost-ofsetting family programs that help families save money, thus increasing their ability to maintain their budgets or increase savings.

STEP relies completely on privately donated funds to execute its mission. Since 2012, STEP has raised and spent more than $3 million to assist 2,500 young, military families out of a verifiable financial crisis and onto a path of financial self-sufficiency, issued $1.1 million in grants to lenders and creditors on behalf of our young military families, and distributed $600,000 of donated goods and services to an additional 5,000 miliary family members. Our grants ensure that our military families do not have to go without a basic need while they are getting their financial situation back on track. Our counsleing empowers them to take ownership of their financial future, giving them a sense of ownership and independence on their financial path. STEP gives each family requesting assitance personalized financial counseling and education which they need to survive over the long run, as well as the immediate relief from an eminant financial crisis. 89 percent of families who receive a grant from STEP do not return for a second allowed assist.

Introduction to the Emergency Financial Assistance Program

The Emergency Financial Assistance (EFA) program is the backbone for all services provided at STEP. The EFA program provides financial counseling and, when necessary, financial grants to military servicemembers and veterans who are currently experiencing a financial crisis. Young military personnel and their families face many of the same financial management challenges as civilians. Like most young adults, they must continually grapple with everyday financial decisions like budgeting and bill paying while also managing long-term considerations like retirement planning and debt management.

However, being in the military also involves unique circumstances and stresses that can make financial management even more difficult. For active duty military families, the frequent moves, the variable availability of Base housing, the difficulty spouses face in finding employment after each move, and the relatively low pay in the junior enlisted ranks combined with Southern California's high cost of living, all create additional financial strain. Frequent family moves are often overlooked as a major souce of financial stress, but STEP client data shows that of the EFA applicants, 65% have moved within the past 24 months, 42% have moved within the past 12 months, and 25% have moved within the past 6 months.

Nationally, nearly 50 percent of veterans try to stay in the city in which they discharge from service. These veteran families, facing the difficult process of transitioning to civilian life, find that Veteran Benefits and G.I. Bill stipends are delayed, unemployment is high, and spouse employment is still very difficult. When these factors combine with the high cost of living in San Diego, young military and veteran families can easily find themselves in a financial crisis. In Southern California, there are 25,000 service members that transition to become veterans each year. Los Angeles and San Diego rank 1st and 3rd respectively in veteran population, and San Diego County has the highest concentration of veterans under the age of 25 in the nation.

STEP's EFA program is designed to assist these families through counseling and grants, not loans. The grants issued never need to be repaid by the families; in fact, all STEP services are free to its clients. STEP works with the family to review their budget and help determine how and why the crisis occurred and get each family on a positve budget path. Then, if necessary to restore or preclude the loss of a basic necessity, STEP issues payments directly to the landlord, utility company, bank, or other appropriate entities. About half of all EFA clients will require, and be issued a grant. STEP also works closely with local mechanics to help ensure families have reliable trasportation, and issues gift cards to local grocery stores or the Base Commissary to ensure families can pay for food. Through these direct payments totalling over $1.1 million, STEP's Emergency Financial Assistance program helped families meet a number of basic needs:

> ➤ 727 struggling families received 2-weeks' food

> ➤ 292 families avoided utility shut offs or had services reinstated

➢ 265 family evictions have been stopped

➢ 240 family car repossessions have been stopped

➢ 112 family vehicles received critical repairs

STEP also helps with vehicle insurance, critical baby items, dental emergencies, emergency travel and other financial hardships that put families in a financial crisis.

STEP's Intended Impact

The intended impact of the EFA program is that military and veteran families will move from financial crisis to financial self-sufficiency through a combination of counseling, education, and resources that help them pay their bills and/or offset their costs of living.

Because financial self-sufficiency is the singularly most important intended impact for STEP, we focused all of our research efforts toward determining whether our client families had achieved some level of self-sufficiency after receiving services from STEP. We recognize that a client has achieved financial self-sufficiency when they are independently capable of meeting their financial needs, accept ownership for their financial situations, and take specific steps to improve their situations.

We developed a number of indicators that would reveal whether our clients had achieved financial self-sufficiency. Using the Dialogues In Action "Heart Triangle" model we identified indicators that would reveal both surface-level changes as well as deeper, life-altering transformation. We then studied the extent to which our clients had achieved those indicators of impact. Our indicators of impact were as follows:

1. They know the next step they need to take to get on the path towards self-sufficiency

2. They feel reduced financial stress

3. They implement one or more financial self-sufficiency skills

4. They believe in and assume ownership of their financial future

5. They are committed to healthy financial future

6. They become stewards of their financial future

Both our qualitative and quantitative protocols were designed with these indicators and our overall intended impact of financial self-sufficiency in mind. Our qualitative interview protocol and survey instrument can be found in the Appendix.

Methodology

We used a combination of qualitative and quantitative data to assess the quality of our impact and the extent to which clients demonstrated any of the six indicators of impact above. We utilized a short, quantitative survey instrument to assess whether former clients reported any surface-level emotional or behavioral changes since working with STEP (Indicators 1-3). We utilized in-depth qualitative interviews in order to understand former clients' current financial lives and whether any lasting transformations had occurred with respect to their financial self-sufficiency (Indicators 4-6).

Qualitative Methodology

We aimed to complete 15-18 interviews with clients along three different sampling criteria: a combination of both active duty and veteran clients, married and single clients, and clients who had receieved a grant and counseling under the EFA program as well as clients who had received counseling only, without a grant. We generated a random list of clients who had received our services at least four months but not more than twelve months in the past, and contacted them by phone to ask for interviews. Like most of our service interventions, all of our interviews were conducted by phone. The interviews typically lasted between 30 and 45 minutes.

We immediately faced an issue with connecting to clients. Former clients were not likely to take our call, and we left several unreturned voicemails. When we did speak with former clients we were delighted that many were willing to be interviewed. However, it was difficult to ensure that the client would follow through with their scheduled interview time. In other words, it was difficult to connect with former clients at all, let alone multiple times to schedule and conduct our interviews. There are several potential reasons for this disconnect, including the fact that STEP works with a population that is often moving around the country and changing their contact information. Despite these challenges, we were able to garner a sample of 8 in-depth interviews with former clients.

Quantitative Methodology

We devised an anonymous, nine-question electronic survey that we sent to every client whom we had assisted from November 2015 through May 2016. The survey was intentionally short; we wanted to assure former clients that participating in the survey would be fast, user friendly, and painless. We sent the survey to clients for whom at least four months had transpired since receiving services from STEP. This was to mitigate potential biases that may result from having worked with STEP too recently, including the emotional (positive or negative) feelings toward a particular case manager or staff and the potential fallout (positive or negative) from receiving a grant. We decided that four months was an appropriate amount of time for our former clients' lives to return to normal, thereby providing a window to see our impacts.

We distributed our survey electronically using the iContacts software tool. We sent email notifications with links to the survey three times. We received 17 responses, with a response rate of seven percent. This response rate is consistent with other follow-up surveys that we have sent to clients in the past.

STEP's Theory of Change

Before reviewing our findings from the qualitative and quantitative data, it is important that we highlight our Theory of Change in order to put our findings in perspective. STEP utilizes a number of social work principles and theories both in the design of our program as well as in the implementation of our procedures and in our interactions with clients. We operate on a social work model that utilizes a solution-focused approach with an emphasis on clients' strengths. The solution-focused approach is an evidence-based practice in the field of social work. The foundation of the solution-focused approach is that the best clinical interventions are relatively brief and goal-oriented in ways that build on the client's strengths. It focuses on what the client wants to achieve, previous successes they have had, and immediate steps they can take in the future to achieve their goal.

Many of our findings are consistent with the solution-focused model that we have built into our program and case management procedures.

In addition, we also have five principles behind our practices that inform our programs and our choice of the solution-focused approach. Those are:

1. **The client is the expert of their own circumstance.** They are the only ones who can tell us what they want to achieve and how they can achieve it.

2. **Relationships are the foundation for change.** By building relationships with clients and facilitating the relationships in their lives, we can help them achieve the changes they want for themselves.

3. **Crisis creates openness.** The existence of a crisis (financial or otherwise) opens up a client to new perspectives and information to which they may not have been open before.

4. **Scarcity of resources facilitates ownership.** The awareness that they cannot repeatedly seek financial grants from STEP (twice in a lifetime limit) encourages the client to take ownership of their situation and learn to act independently.

5. **Emergency grants (helping clients "break even") creates an environment for financial success.** Clients will not be successful if they need to keep spending their limited money to get themselves out of a financial hole; financial grants provide just enough to get

the client back on their feet so that they can start building a better financial future for themselves.

We were happy to discover that most of our findings, even the most surprising ones, were somehow connected to the solution-focused approach or the theory of change principles that STEP has intentionally built into its program.

Limitations of Findings

Several factors limit our ability to generalize our findings to make broad and conclusive statements about STEP's impact. These include:

Small sample sizes and low response rates: the lack of interview and survey responsiveness means that we have derived our findings from a very narrow proportion of the population with which STEP has worked in the past year.

1. Interview versus survey responses: because the survey responses were anonymous, we have no way to know who took the survey and whether there was overlap in these respondents. However, due to our small sample sizes, overlap is possible but not probable.

2. Selection biases: Our sample has two potential selection biases:

   a. Active duty clients make up a signficiant proportion of our sample. While they are not overrepresented relative to our client population, there is not as much veteran representation in the sample as we originally planned.

   b. Clients who received financial grants and counseling (versus clients who received counseling without a grant) are overrepresented in our sample.

3. Team limitations and time constraints: due to limitations in manpower and resources, much of the data collection was conducted by one team member, and thus there may be some potential researcher bias in the interpretation of the data.

Findings:

Despite the limitations of our data, we found seven remarkable trends among our former clients. These findings communicate to us what we are doing well and how STEP might improve as we continue to grow and refine our program into the future. We are also reminded about the pressing external factors that take a significant toll in the lives of our active-duty and veteran families.

Finding 1: *Where Are They Now? - Client Engagement After STEP*

Our difficulty in reaching our former clients was the first indicator that clients may not feel very engaged with STEP and therefore do not maintain or seek to maintain contact with us after they have received assistance. The low response rate in both the survey and our requests for interviews communicate that clients may not feel a strong emotional relationship with STEP. In addition, every client who was interviewed was unable to name the case manager with whom they worked when they went through STEP's Emergency Financial Assistance program.

This finding is significant because it forced us to evaluate whether we found the lack of engagement acceptable as we move forward as an organization. On one hand, our focus on brief, solution-focused interventions do not encourage repeated follow-ups nor sustained connections with clients; we want the clients to get what they can from us and move on with their lives. On the other hand, we want clients to know that they can still reach out to us in the future if they want to receive financial counseling due to a change in circumstances or a desire to re-work their budgets. This finding illuminates that we can and should be more aware about the level of engagement we want and expect from former clients so that we can set clearer goals for the organization as it grows.

Finding 2: *Crisis Averted - STEP is Influential in Times of Crisis*

Virtually all of our interview respondents stressed how helpful STEP was in helping them during what was a very stressful and fearful moment of their lives. Many of them indicated that without the financial assistance in paying a particular bill or expense, they don't know what they would have done or where they would have turned.

> I just wanted to let you know I am very appreciative of the STEP program and the ease to get help. When I went to other organizations for help, they weren't as friendly with me.

> We really got ourselves into a bad spot and you guys were there for us in a way no one else was. It was really good timing because we were, like literally, running out of money.

> Well you guys helped us a lot with that grant, so we were able to have one less thing to worry about. I think that helped us focus on other things to pay down and then it was just good to have less stress for a while.

This was one of the most encouraging trends in our data. STEP's goal is to help east the financial strain of military and veteran families who are facing an imminent financial crisis and to help them move toward financial self-suffienciency. This finding reveals that we are meeting our goal of assisting them in crisis and, when combined with our other findings, suggest that it is a crucial component of building financial self-sufficiency in our clients.

Finding 3: *Breathing Easier - STEP is Influential in Reducing Financial Stress*

One of our indicators of impact would be that clients would feel reduced financial stress as a result of working with STEP. This indicator was strongly confirmed in our survey data.

We asked survey respondents to rate their level of financial stress before working with STEP on a scale from zero to five, with zero indicating "no stress" and five indicating "very high stress." None of the survey respondents rated their "before" level of stress as a zero, one, or two (no stress, very low stress, or some stress); everyone rated their "before" stress level as a three, four, or five (moderate stress, high stress, very high stress). Over half of our respondents reported their "before" stress level as a five – very high stress.

Rate your financial stress *before* you came to STEP

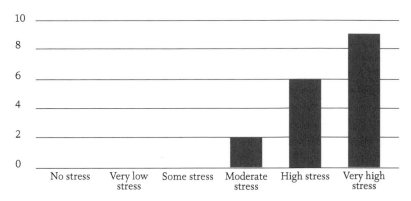

Rate your financial stress *now*, as a result of working with STEP

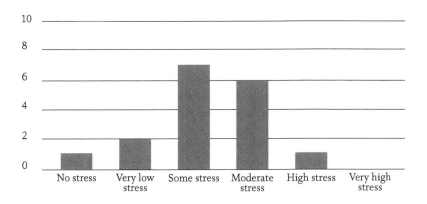

When we asked survey respondents to rate their financial stress now as a result of working with STEP, we saw a drastic reduction in the reported levels of stress. Whereas not a single respondent rated their "before" stress level as a zero, one, or two, over half of the respondents rated their "now" stress level in these categories. While half of our respondents reported their "before" stress level as a five – very high stress, none of these respondents rated their current stress levels as high.

The mean "before" stress level for our survey respondents was a 4.18 out of 5. The mean "now" stress level was a 2.29 out of 5. These survey responses indicate that STEP was able to reduce clients' financial stress by 45%. It is difficult to rationalize a 45% stress reduction, but when utilizing the scale used in the survey, we find that the mean stress levels were reduced from between High and Very High to between Some and Moderate. This is a significant finding not only because it helps us confirm that we are achieving one of our indicators of impact, but because it gets to the heart of why STEP was founded in the first place.

Finding 4: *"Thank You," but not "Thanks to You" - Clients Explicit and Implied Reporting of Impact*

A surprising finding that challenged our assumptions came through our qualitative interviews. During these discussions, many of the clients we spoke with offered up sincere gratitude for the assistance they received and talked about how their current financial situations had improved in the time since they originally came to STEP. However, these same clients did not attribute their reduced stress or improved financial state to the financial skills or budget help they received at STEP. Many could not even recall receiving these kinds of counseling services from STEP at all.

> I don't really remember learning anything in particular. It was just such a relief that we got a grant that we didn't have to pay back.

> I don't remember the education. I found you guys through Google because we were living in a house that was not financially responsible and we got behind on our rent, and you guys got us squared up on that. But in terms of teaching or training I didn't really get any of that.

While many clients did not explicitly credit STEP with their reduced financial stress or more stable financial life, we did see a curious subtext in the interviews that we found interesting. The same respondents who claimed that STEP was not the most important factor in improving their financial life were also talking about their budgets, debt-reduction, and saving plans in very specific and concrete terms, using the same or similar goals and benchmarks that STEP uses in its financial counseling. When most clients come into STEP, they claim to have budgets but to not use them or even know where to find them, or claim to want to save but to not know how. By contrast, our interview respondents could offer relatively concrete and coherent strategies that they are using to achieve greater financial success. For example, respondents talked about how they sit down with their spouses to work out the budget, many of them talking about the specific time period, frequency, and strategies that go into their budget planning. Another respondent was able to offer a very precise benchmark for his emergency savings fund – $10,000 – the same figure that STEP uses when teaching about emergency savings funds. Other respondents used precise language as well:

> Well we are paying our bills on time, which is good. We keep an electronic budget, we just put everything into an Excel spreadsheet. So my husband and I both have fixed paychecks so we put everything in and see where the money is going, and we decide how to pay down debt and save, and we make sure we aren't maxing out on anything.

> Well, we have learned that it is pretty important to have a savings account set aside especially when going underway or deploying. The lady my wife talked to when this whole thing happened suggested we needed to have like $13,000 set aside for emergencies. So, that's definitely the goal, but it's pretty hard to obtain.

Unfortunately, our survey data cannot speak to this trend in the interviews. While, most of our survey respondents agreed that they had learned at least one skill for improving their finances, we did not explicitly ask survey respondents whether or not learning those skills contributed to their reduced financial stress.

While we do not mean to imply that our clients are wrong in not crediting STEP, nor to put words into their mouths by pointing out the things that were implied but not said, this finding is still significant to us. At minimum, this finding is instructive for how we should be engaging and interacting with clients during and even after giving them financial counseling. We want to be making sure to drive home the specific and concrete goals with our clients because that is what they are most likely to remember. We also want to reinforce to them several times how much they have learned and the growth they have been able to achieve in our program, so that they can remember not just that STEP helped them, but also how STEP helped them.

Finding 5: *Baby STEPs - Everyone is on a Path They Believe will Pay Off*

Both the interview and survey data confirmed that virtually all of our respondents are focusing on a specific skill or habit to improve their financial situation and that they have a clear financial goal toward which they are working. Many of our interview respondents discussed a desire to spend less, and cited specific areas where they have reduced their spending.

> I live with the bare minimum now. If I don't need something, I won't get it. I also cut down on things for a while, like cable, until I was able to afford it.

> I think we are just trying to be more aware of how we are spending our money. You know, trying not to eat McDonald's as much, and instead of McDonalds its like, "hey, let's just make some sandwiches at home." We are trying to make it so that we don't have to go out for things as much.

Other interview respondents commented on other skills, such as budgeting, and innovative strategies, such as wisely spending tax refunds, that they are using to build a healthier financial life.

> Even though you maintain a budget, I'm just sending more to savings rather than spending it on stuff. I'm just paranoid all the time about having something happen and not having a contingency plan. Savings, savings, savings. We try not to ever take any money out of there.

> I can't stop telling people how important savings is.

> Probably paying down the credit card bills has been the best thing, and using that money towards savings so that we can buy a house, hopefully sometime this year.

These findings are confirmed in our survey responses. When asked the question, "As a result of working with STEP, what step(s) have you taken to improve your financial future," three quarters of respondents report that they are working to pay down or reduce their debts, and over half of these respondents are focusing on maintaining a positive account balance and paying their bills on time.

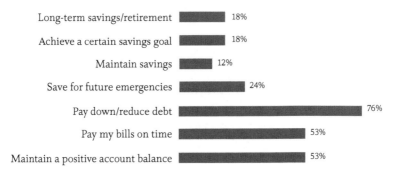

Both our interviews and our surveys confirm that saving is one of the primary financial goals towards which our former clients are working. The importance of saving was repeated time and again during our interview discussions. When survey respondents were asked about their next step or goal for improving their financial futures, 55 percent of them specifically cited savings in their response.

We are inspired by this finding that everyone in our sample is using some kind of skill to improve their financial life and can clearly identify a financial goal for themselves. This finding confirms three of our six indicators of financial self-sufficiency: that clients will know the next step they need to take to get on the path towards self-sufficiency, that they implement one or more financial self-sufficiency skills, and that they are committed to healthy financial future.

Finding 6: *Still on Edge - Many Families Still Face Hard Financial Times*

Despite the overall reduction in financial stress, many of the former clients we interviewed report that times are still tough. A few of our respondents talked about regularly fearing and narrowly avoiding financial catastrophe.

We are surviving but it's been hard. It's been a bad year. It's been really hard since my husband retired.

We still have plenty of moments that knock us down. I call them "Oh, sh*t" moments. We have so many of those but we are trying.

You know, we got the help we needed and it got us through a tough time. Now we are facing another tough time, another situation

Still more of the interviews revolved around discussion of new problems and specific obstacles that inhibit clients' abilities to live the financial lives they want. Issues with creditors, making payments on vehicles, the cost of childcare, and high costs of living were all significant themes.

One of our interview respondents is currently in the process of applying to STEP for a second grant, claiming that life is still very difficult for his family and that it doesn't take much to knock them into a state of crisis. He said: "You try to do the best you can, but if there's no money then that's it. Like, our dog got sick and that totally threw us off. That's a tough spot to be in."

Even among our respondents who are doing much better financially, they reference the struggles they had to endure to get to that place and how difficult it was. They spoke of not wanting to "go back" to the time when they felt as if they were at the end of their ropes. While their stories inspire us, they also enlighten us to the fact that many of our former clients are not yet where they want to be and may be in need of both personal success plans as well as available community resources.

Stand By Me: Military and Societal Issues Take Their Toll on Military/Veteran Families

Throughout our interviews, we consistently learned about some of the pressing external problems that take their toll on our clients and their families. First, a consistent theme in the interview data was how the cost of living in San Diego (or Southern California more broadly) made life extremely difficult for military and veteran families, who often have little or no choice about living there. Two of our interview respondents went so far as to say that they don't know whether they would have survived if they had not moved out of state.

> Honestly I don't think we would have survived if we stayed in California. Because everything there is so much more expensive. The cost of living [in Louisiana] is so much better, honestly.

> We moved into a military housing community so that has helped a lot. The BAH goes directly to our rent and we don't have to pay utilities. So we are doing pretty good in terms of paying bills on time, because of how much the military housing has saved us compared to the high costs off Base.

Another theme in the data was the importance of affordable housing and manageable commutes from home to Base for active duty respondents. Respondents noted that getting into Base housing was crucial for maintaining their budgets, reducing debt, and building savings. Yet Base housing is not always available and there are often waiting lists and hierarchies for who gets approved for Base housing. Without Base housing, many respondents face the added cost (in money and time) of having to commute long distances to and from work every day. One respondent talked at length about how she had to commute between her home and two different bases an average of 120 miles per day. Not only did this take up all her time, it exhausted her vehicle and her wallet.

Finally, several of our respondents discussed issues with credit and the difficulty they faced in dealing with auto lenders and credit card companies. One of our clients spoke about how she was "praying every day" that a credit company would refinance their auto loan so that they could afford the monthly payments. Another spoke about how she was relying on credit cards to buy food for her family, and the only way to get out of this debt was to devote her reenlistment bonus to paying it off. These issues with creditors are not surprising to us; military personnel often have complicated credit histories. What is surprising to us is the extent to which issues with credit might be preventing our clients from reaching their long-term financial goals.

While all of these issues are beyond the scope of STEP, we recognize that we are an advocate for the military and veteran community, and that it is our obligation to use our platform to make sure these issues are well known. That means communicating these findings to our Board, to local advisory councils, and to other advocates and policy makers.

Implications and Recommendations

These findings are not only insightful to the quality of our impact, they also point out areas where we can make some strategic adjustments to make sure that STEP continues to have a positive impact in the community and to grow this impact as we continue to grow as an organization. These findings also come at a moment when we are about to review and update our client services procedures, and we intend to integrate these findings into that process. Based on what we have learned from this research process, we intend to explore the feasibility making the following adjustments at STEP.

Client Services

The finding that clients are likely to be grateful for STEP, yet not necessarily credit STEP for their reduced financial stress or the very specific and concrete financial skills that they are using, encourages us to improve the way we are communicating our program to our clients. We want them to recognize that they have learned and grown after working with STEP. We would like to stress the following in our engagement with clients:

> ➤ Encourage clients to understand how far they have come since they first called STEP.

> ➤ Build into the case management and counseling very specific, concrete, and memorable steps and financial goals/benchmarks.

> ➤ Reinforce the process by which they've learned these skills

We also want to slightly adjust the level of engagement we retain with former clients while still staying committed to our solution-focused brief therapy approach. To do this we intend to make the following adjustments:

➢ Add some follow-up questions after the intervention is complete to keep the relationship positive and intact.

➢ Stress to clients that returning to STEP for budget counseling whenever they need it will not count against the twice in a lifetime limit.

➢ Consider following-up with people 1-3 months after the intervention to touch base.

We will discuss these recommended changes with our board and staff and use them as guides when revising the client services procedures and refreshing the case managers' training.

Advocacy

We want to share our findings with relevant parties who can assist us in being advocates for the military and veteran families in our community as well as across the nation. This includes talking to active duty military commands, veterans groups, and our community partners about the issues that continue to affect these families. We intend to do the following to communicate our findings widely:

➢ Feature them extensively in the Support The Enlisted Project Annual Report, which is read not only by STEP Board members but also funders, grant makers, and other parties with a vested interest in military and veteran issues.

➢ Have a special "Project Impact" presentation at our next Board of Directors meeting, many of whom are advocates for the military.

➢ Present our findings and experiences to the San Diego Military Advisory Council, the San Diego Veterans Coalition, and the San Diego Military Family Collaborative.

➤ Discuss these findings during our community outreach to military commands, family readiness officers, and ombudsmen.

Conclusions

Participation in the Project Impact research process has clarified our articulation of our impacts and yielded several important insights into the quality of the impact STEP is having in the community we serve. We have not only learned how to design and implement these data collection methods, we also have a plan for how to sustain both qualitative and quantitative data collection into the future. We have learned that while it is difficult to connect with our former clients, once we do they have several positive things to say, including that we offered crucial support during times of crisis and that we reduced their financial stress dramatically. Even if they cannot explicitly credit STEP with current financial wellness levels, we are encouraged that clients are retaining some of the more specific goals that we stress during our solution-focused interventions and that everyone is taking at least some small step towards achieving their financial goals. However, our work is far from over. Many of these families still face dire financial situations, which are often made worse by military and society problems beyond their and our control. By implementing these insights into our program and advocacy efforts, we are optimistic that STEP will continue to have a positive impact in the military and veteran community. We are committed to serving them, because they have committed to serving our country.

Appendix

Qualitative Interview Protocols

Words Alive
Student Interview

Know → Believe

What has being a part of Words Alive taught you about the importance of reading? → How has reading changed the way you think? Or perceive the world?

How has Words Alive helped you in seeing out information? How has this helped you be better able to make connections to text and real like applications? → What does knowledge mean to you now?

What are the most meaningful things you learned from the development workshops? → How have the development workshops -- like Share Your Story -- changed the way you see your future?

Do → Become

What barriers to reading regularly have you overcome based on what you've learned from the Words Alive book club? → How have you remained engaged in reading as a result?

What skills have you learned from Words Alive to become a better reader? → In what ways has reading become a part of your daily life? → How has reading improved your life?

In what ways are you able to better express yourself clearly through writing after Words Alive? ➙ Has Words Alive helped you in defining your voice? If yes, how?

Feel ➙Love

In what ways has Words Alive changed the way you feel about reading? How has this inspired you? ➙ After participating in the Words Alive Program, how are you more empowered to invest in your future?

How comfortable are you now in navigating post-secondary and career systems? ➙ How has this changed your commitment to your future success?

What has been difficult for you to do in achieving your personal, educational or career goals? What do you consider to be your greatest accomplishment/achievement this school year? ➙ How have these experiences made you more passionate about living your dreams?

Teacher Interview

Know ➙ Believe

What has being a part of Words Alive taught your students about the importance of reading? How have student discussion dynamics and their reactions to tests changed as ABG sessions progress? ➙ How has reading changed the way your students think or perceive their world?

How has Words Alive helped your students seek out information? ➙How has this helped your students be better able to make connections to text and real life applications?

Do➙Become

What barriers to reading regularly have you witnessed your students overcome based on what they've learned from the Words Alive book club? ➙ How have they remained engaged in reading as a result?

What skills have you seen your students learn from Words Alive to become better readers? ➙ In what ways has reading become a part of their daily lives? ➙How have you seen reading improve your students' lives?

In what ways are your students better able to express themselves clearly through writing after Words Alive? → Has Words Alive helped your students define their voices? If yes, how?

What student reading achievement are you most proud this school year? In what areas are your students struggling to apply the things they've learned? What been difficult to do? → What still needs to develop in your students to make progress the way you hope?

Feel→Love

How has Words Alive changed the way your students feel about reading? How has this inspired them? In what ways do they still feel discouraged about reading? → How has Words Alive changed the way you use books and reading in your classroom? How has Words Alive impacted your classroom/teaching goals regarding Language Arts?

Just in Time for Foster Youth

Know → Believe

What have been some of the most useful lessons you've learned from Pathways about achieving financial security? → How does what you know now affect your belief about your ability to reach your financial goals? How has your commitment to your own success gotten stronger?

What have you learned from Pathways about how your past experiences and assumptions have affected your current views and expectations about relationships? What healthy connections have you made after understanding that effect? → At what point did you start to believe that relationships could make your life better? How do you believe trusting connections have changed your life?

What have you discovered about yourself through recognizing and using your strengths? What about them makes you feel most optimistic about for your future? What concepts are you still working to understand? → How have those qualities helped you move forward in the face of discouragement? What do you value about yourself that has changed your outlook on the key challenges in your life?

Do → Become

What skills and behaviors did you need to start or improve to move toward your long term goals? How were these developed through this program? → In what ways have those changes given you a new set of motivations? How has your financial confidence made other parts of your life different?

What were some self-limiting things you used to do, if any, before Pathways? What has Pathways helped you do to work on those limits? What assumptions are you still struggling to overcome? → What inner strengths are you able to tap into now to create the future you want? How will you make your life different because of your strengths?

As a result of Pathways, what steps would you take now to overcome an obstacle or a major challenge? What do you do now that you wouldn't have done before? → How is your life different now that you have embraced this approach? What changes in you have others noticed and told you about?

What have been the most significant barriers you've worked to overcome during your experience with Pathways? What opportunities have you acted on? What did you achieve? What have you not yet achieved that you've been hoping to? → How has your capacity to face difficulties and succeed grown as a result? How has that changed the way you will approach your future?

Feel → Love

What are groups or communities you've joined as a result of Pathways that give you a feeling of support and belonging? → What makes you most deeply passionate about those connections? How do you show attachment to the group/community and create even stronger bonds?

What has been the most exciting part of having a voice? What energizes you the most? → How has this change consistently affected you each week? What does it take to keep your voice strong when situations or people discourage you from speaking out?

What are some of the key ideas about yourself or things that matter to you that frustrated you most in the past? What ideas or principles are you eager to express now? → What personal values are you able to express now with confidence and passion, even when it's difficult? What drives you to advocate for others, even when it may take you outside your comfort zone?

Olivewood Gardens

What new cooking techniques or practices have you implemented based on what you've learned in Cooking for Salud? → How have your habits changed as a result of what you've learned?

What skills that you learned in Cooking for Salud are you using when you go to the grocery store? → How has what you've learned motivated you to evaluate what you purchase?

What was the most surprising discovery you made about your diet when you were in the class? → How did this discovery led you to think differently about the food you eat?

What does meal planning and preparation look like for your family? How has the way you plan and prepare meals with your family changed as a result of Cooking for Salud? → In what way has this transformed your family dynamic?

What changes have you made to engage your children in the cooking process? → In what ways have your new kitchen routines affected your children's overall well-being?

How are your ideas and your family's ideas about healthy food different now than compared to before you took the class? → How has this affected you and the way your family values health?

What emotions do you experience when you make a healthy meal? What makes you feel most proud? → How does that feeling shape your commitment to continuing this journey?

What has been frustrating and what excites you about implementing these changes at home? → What essential changes are you committed to making despite the difficulties/occasional setbacks?

What have you learned about yourself through this process? → What do you believe you can do next? What do you think you're capable of achieving?

How have the stories of the other Kitchenistas resonated with you? → What is it about this community that has given you the courage to make changes and persevere through challenges?

Pro Kids| The First Tee of San Diego

What have you learned about the key beliefs at Pro Kids? What personal values of yours are in common with the Pro Kids? → How have your personal values changed since joining Pro Kids? *(Know- Believe)*

What have you learned at Pro Kids that's been most helpful to you? →How does this impact your life at home and school? *(Know- Believe)*

What beliefs did you hold that limited your ability to be a good student before this program? → How do you see your future differently you started the academy? *(Know- Believe)*

What makes you feel most successful at Pro Kids? → How has this shaped or influenced what you want your life to be about? *(Feel – Love)*

What is most exciting about your team? → "How do you appreciate yourself differently than you used to?" *(Feel – Love)*

What is most frustrating to you about your team? →What keeps you committed to this even when it's hard? How have you been growing in your ability to stick with the tough but good commitments in your life? *(Feel – Love)*

What is your most frequently experienced emotion you feel at Pro Kids → How has that affected your commitment to reaching your potential in other parts of your life? *(Feel – Love)*

What skills have you developed since being a part of the Academy? → How have these been applied in other areas of your life and school? *(Do- Become)*

What tasks have you struggled with the most or found most challenging? → What needed/needs to change in you to be able overcome struggles and challenges? *(Do- Become)*

What do you consistently try to do now that you weren't able to do before you joined the academy? → How were you able to come to a place where you could do this differently? *(Do-Become)*

Hospice of the North Coast

What have been some of the biggest lessons you learned through this process? → What has been most meaningful and supported you to grow as a person?

How has what you learned in bereavement counseling helped you process your grief? → How has bereavement counseling enabled you to change your thoughts about dying and loss?

What have you discovered about the way you handle grief during your therapy? → How has this brought you closer to accepting your loss?

What choices have you made since starting bereavement counseling that have added a new dimension to your life? What choices are you still struggling with? → How have those choices changed the way you perceive your future after your loss?

What activities have you begun in your daily life, which have helped to resolve your grief? What does resolution of grief look like to you? → How is that manifest in your life?

What has been difficult for you to do in this process? What skills have you developed to help with this? What skills do you still need to develop? → How has that shaped the way you approach life's challenges?

What are the 3 most significant feelings of grief you've been able to identify through bereavement counseling? What about bereavement counseling brings you hope? →How has this shaped what you are passionate about in life?

What has made you most proud in this process? → How has that helped you to stay committed through the tough parts?

What supportive relationships have you developed as a result of bereavement counseling? → How has this made you feel more connected to yourself and others?

Venice Family Clinic

Know - Believe

In the past few months, what have you learned about your health from VFC? What's been the most meaningful to you? → How are you thinking differently about your health?

What have you learned from VFC about how to care for yourself? → How has this changed the way you view your role in your health care?

What have you learned about accessing services at VFC? → What do you believe now about your potential for good health?

Do-Become

In the past few months, how has VFC helped you set and/or achieve your health goals? → How has your ability to care for your health changed as a result? How has your motivation to care for yourself changed?

What changes have you made to how you care for yourself/your health? → How have these changes/successes improved other aspects of your life?

What health challenges/successes have you faced in caring for yourself since coming to VFC? → How has VFC helped you to build on these successes and challenges to improve your health? How have your family/friends seen you differently as a result?

Feel-Love

In the past few months, what skills have you used to manage your health? → How are you becoming the best/healthiest version of yourself?

What are you most proud of (or do you cherish most) about your health? → How has this changed your dreams of good health in the future?

What connections have you made as a result of getting services at VFC? → How have these connections/support shaped your commitment to your health?

What concerns you about your future health? What excites you? →How has this changed how you will face health challenges in the future?

Support the Enlisted Project

What were the most useful things you learned through this program? → How has this made you think about your life (or your family) differently? (**Know-Believe**)

What have you learned about financial goal setting? → How has this changed what you believe is possible for you/your family's financial future? (**Know-Believe**)

How has your ability to pay bills on time changed as a result of this program? → How have you changed your lifestyle to make this possible? (**Do-Become**)

What has been the most exciting part of maintaining your budget? → How have those kinds of things made you more committed to your financial goals? (**Feel-Love**)

What has been the most stressful part of maintaining your budget? → How do you stay motivated to maintain your budget during those times when you're feeling stressed? (**Feel-Love**)

Before being part of this program, what were your biggest fears when you thought about your finances? → How have you cultivated the confidence to stick to your goals in spite of those fears? (**Feel-Love**)

What is a skill you have implemented that you wish you had learned as a child? → How does this change the way you interact with your children? (**Do-Become**)

What skills have you been talking about with people close to you? → What have they noticed has changed in you as a result of this program? (**Do-Become**)

Over the next 2-3 years, what do you want to accomplish financially? → How do you want your life to be different as a result of this program? (**Do-Become**)

Made in the USA
San Bernardino, CA
28 December 2017